The Anxiety Antidote

Natural Remedies to Soothe Your Mind and Body

Michelle Mann

Copyright © 2024 by Michelle Mann

All rights reserved.

No portion of this book may be reproduced in any form without written permission from the publisher or author, except as permitted by U.S. copyright law.

Contents

1. Introduction — 1
2. Illuminating Paths of Hope in Understanding Anxiety — 5
3. Anxiety and the Mind-Body Connection — 27
4. Nourishing the Mind — 32
5. Embracing Serenity — 54
6. Nurturing Harmony — 79
7. Nurturing Tranquility — 88
8. Embracing Hope — 99
9. Nurturing Your Path to Lasting Serenity — 124

Introduction

In the soothing rhythm of life, where our existence harmonizes with the gentle notes of our emotions, anxiety often weaves its way into the fabric of our hearts. This book, "The Anxiety Antidote: Natural Remedies to Soothe Your Mind and Body," is a haven, more than a mere collection of words. It stands as a sanctuary of calm, a refuge crafted with profound empathy and understanding for those navigating the currents of anxiety in our fast-paced world.

The Modern Tapestry of Anxiety

Imagine the modern world as an expansive tapestry, woven with threads of diverse experiences and challenges. In this intricate masterpiece, anxiety seamlessly intertwines itself, affecting many in varying degrees. From the subtle rustling of unease accompanying everyday stress to the more pronounced shadows of chronic worry, anxiety's presence reverberates across the spectrum of our society.

Recognizing anxiety's prevalence, the World Health Organization underscores its impact as one of the most widespread mental health conditions globally. Amidst the demands of careers, relationships, and the ceaseless flow of information, anxiety takes root. Its manifestations, diverse and profound, touch our thoughts, emotions, and physical well-being, creating an urgent need for strategies that are not only effective but also accessible and holistic.

The Aim of the Book

Welcome to a journey of exploration and healing. "The Anxiety Antidote" extends a gentle hand to guide you through the nuanced landscape of anxiety, unveiling its impact on your well-being. Our mission is profound yet simple: to empower you with the soothing embrace of natural remedies, drawn from the abundant resources of nature, to bring solace to your mind and body in the face of life's challenges.

This book is not a claim to instant solutions but a roadmap, a companion on your journey towards well-being. In a world often clamoring for quick fixes, we advocate for a holistic and sustainable approach. The remedies within these pages are not mere interventions; they are companions inviting you to forge a profound connection with yourself and the world around you. From the tender touch of acupressure to the aromatic embrace of essential oils, from the therapeutic balm of nature therapy to the rhythmic pathway of emotional freedom technique tapping, these remedies honor the unique path each individual treads.

Types of Natural Remedies Covered:

As we gently unfurl the pages ahead, envision a tapestry of natural remedies carefully woven to contribute to the symphony of well-being. Delve into the ancient practices of acupressure and acupuncture, exploring the subtle dance of energy within your body. Let aromatherapy, with its captivating scents, be an invitation to immerse yourself in the fragrant world of essential oils. Allow nature therapy to beckon you towards rediscovering the healing embrace of the natural world, while tapping, rooted in ancient wisdom and modern psychology, offers a rhythmic pathway to emotional freedom.

Beyond these, we explore dietary adjustments, lifestyle changes, mindfulness practices, and alternative therapies, forming a rich palette of options. The goal is not to prescribe a one-size-fits-all solution but to encourage a personalized and intuitive approach—an exploration of remedies that resonate with your preferences and needs.

As you embark on this shared journey, remember that healing is not a destination; it's an ongoing evolution—a dance with the ebb and flow of life. "The Anxiety Antidote" invites you to reclaim agency over your well-being, to discover the innate capacity of your mind and body to find balance and serenity. May the remedies within these pages serve as beacons of hope, gently guiding you towards a life where anxiety takes its place not as a dominating force but as a gentle reminder to tend to the sanctuary within.

Illuminating Paths of Hope in Understanding Anxiety

One moment we are walking through our day, and the next, overcome with existential dread for unknown reasons. Our heart pounds uncontrollably, we may feel faint, dizzy, and unable to breathe. We may break out in a cold sweat or feel like we must get away from people. Often feelings of impending death overcome us, and we may even call for emergency services, thinking we are having a heart attack. But, in this case it is not a physical illness, but an equally terrifying panic attack.

In the vast landscape of human emotions, anxiety stands as a complex and intricate facet of our shared experience.

Woven into the fabric of our minds and bodies, it manifests in ways both profound and varied. In this exploration, we embark on a journey to understand anxiety—a journey that unfolds the definition, explores the complex triggers, and underscores the importance of seeking help. Through the lens of compassion and hope, we aim to shed light on anxiety's convolutions, offering a beacon for those navigating its depths.

Understanding anxiety requires a nuanced exploration that transcends the mere acknowledgment of its existence. Anxiety is more than a passing emotion; it is a dynamic force that impacts thoughts, emotions, and the very physiology of our beings. As we delve into the multifaceted nature of anxiety, we uncover not only the challenges it poses but also the potential for growth, resilience, and healing.

Defining Anxiety

Anxiety, in its essence, is a natural response—a guardian alerting us to potential stress and threats. Psychologically, it weaves feelings of apprehension and worry, while physiologically, it orchestrates the dance of stress hormones like cortisol and adrenaline. This coordinated effort, often recognized as the "fight or flight" response, manifests physically through increased heart rate, shallow breathing, muscle tension, and more. In ancient times anxiety kept us alert, aware, and able to run or face our challenges, as needed.

Yet, this natural response can become a challenge when it lingers beyond its intended purpose, evolving into chronic worry that disrupts our daily lives. The clinical diagnosis of Generalized Anxiety Disorder (GAD) encapsulates this prolonged and uncontrollable worry, accompanied by a symphony of physical symptoms.

To truly grasp the essence of anxiety, we must recognize it not as an isolated occurrence but as a continuum, ranging from the ordinary concerns of daily life to the more pronounced symptoms that characterize anxiety disorders. Mild anxiety can serve as a motivational force, prompting us to prepare for challenges, meet deadlines, or navigate social interactions. However, when anxiety transcends its adaptive role and transforms into a persistent, overwhelming force, it necessitates a closer examination.

Psychological Aspects of Anxiety

To grasp anxiety's psychological intricacies is to acknowledge its diverse forms. Anxiety disorders—such as social anxiety, panic disorder, and specific phobias—paint unique portraits of challenges. Social anxiety may cast shadows on social interactions, while panic disorder brings forth unexpected and recurrent panic attacks.

Navigating the spectrum of anxiety disorders unveils a tapestry of unique experiences, each presenting its own set of nuances and hurdles. Consider social anxiety, a gentle reminder of the human inclination to seek connection and understanding. In the realm of social anxiety, individuals grapple with an overwhelming fear of judgment or embarrassment in social scenarios. The prospect of facing these situations can be daunting, prompting some to withdraw, cancel plans, or persist through them with a sense of internal turmoil.

Social anxiety, as with all anxiety, is a spectrum. Most of us have had days where we feel uncomfortable going into a social situation. And we all have canceled plans for good-or no-reason. Pervasive and constant worry of judgement, embarrassment or fear of what others think that interferes with daily life and social events may point to a more serious disorder.

Meanwhile, let's explore panic disorder, a compassionate acknowledgment of the sudden and intense waves of fear that individuals may encounter. Imagine a scenario where a person, in the midst of their daily life, is overcome by palpitations, sweating, and an overwhelming sense of impending doom. These physical manifestations accompany a surge of anxiety, creating a challenging landscape to navigate. It's like facing a tempest within, where the storm clouds gather swiftly, leaving individuals to weather the emotional turbulence.

These experiences with anxiety may leave us exhausted, wrung out emotionally, and even physically sore. Yet, within the folds of these experiences, there exists hope and compassion. In the face of social anxiety, gentle understanding can be extended to those who may find solace in the cancellation of plans or the cautious endurance of social events. These actions are not mere avoidance but rather coping mechanisms in a delicate dance with vulnerability.

Similarly, individuals grappling with panic attacks deserve a nurturing embrace, acknowledging the strength it takes to confront such intense moments of fear. In these moments, a compassionate tone becomes a guiding light, fostering an environment where individuals can journey toward healing and resilience. Panic attacks may not start from a physical threat, but they are terrifying, and they feel as if one is in immediate danger of dying. Understanding this and giving ourselves gentle grace is one step along our healing journey.

In the realm of cognition, distorted thinking patterns, like catastrophizing and perfectionism, shape the landscape of anxiety. Cognitive-behavioral therapy (CBT), a beacon of hope, steps forth to untangle these patterns, guiding individuals toward managing and alleviating their anxiety.

Common distorted thinking patterns

Catastrophizing:

- Distorted Thought: "If I don't get this promotion, my career is over. I'll never be successful, and my life will be a complete failure."

All-or-Nothing Thinking (Black and White Thinking)

- Distorted Thought: "I made a mistake on this project, so I'm a total failure. There's no middle ground; it's either perfect or a disaster."

Overgeneralization:

- Distorted Thought: "I didn't get invited to this social event. I'm always left out. Nobody likes me."

Mind Reading

- Distorted Thought: "My friend didn't call me back. They must be angry with me. I can tell they're upset, even though they didn't say anything."

Personalization:

- Distorted Thought: "My colleague seems stressed today; it must be because of something I did. I always seem to cause problems for others."

Should Statements:

- Distorted Thought: "I should always excel at everything I do. If I make a mistake, I'm a failure."

Labeling and Mislabeling:

- Distorted Thought: "I forgot to send that email; I'm such a careless and irresponsible person. I'm a total failure."

Emotional Reasoning:

- Distorted Thought: "I feel anxious about this situation, so it must be dangerous. My feelings are always accurate indicators of reality."

Discounting the Positive:

- Distorted Thought: "I received compliments on my presentation, but they were just being polite. They didn't really mean it; I'm not good at public speaking."

Selective Abstraction (Focusing on the Negative):

- Distorted Thought: "I received positive feedback on my report, but my boss mentioned one small mistake. I'm a failure because of that one error."

Recognizing oneself in these distorted thoughts is not cause for alarm. The strength of cognitive-behavioral therapy shines through its capacity to uncover and transform unhelpful thought patterns. Take, for instance, someone grappling with social anxiety, carrying unfounded beliefs about being harshly judged by others. With the guidance of CBT, they embark on a journey of recognizing and reshaping these thoughts, replacing them with perspectives that are both realistic and balanced. This transformative process not only eases the immediate distress linked to anxious thoughts but also equips individuals with the tools to approach social situations with increasing confidence and ease over time. Embracing the potential for positive change, CBT offers a reassuring path toward greater mental well-being.

Physiological Aspects of Anxiety

The physiological aspects of anxiety intertwine intimately with the body's stress response. Faced with perceived threats, the body activates the sympathetic nervous system, releasing stress hormones. This biological symphony orchestrates increased heart rate, elevated blood pressure, and rapid breathing—a physiological ballet designed for survival. Yet, in the context of chronic anxiety, this persistent activation can cast shadows on physical health, contributing to cardiovascular issues and more.

Understanding the physiological manifestations of anxiety is crucial for a holistic approach to its management. Chronic activation of the body's stress response, if left unaddressed, can lead to a cascade of health issues. Cardiovascular problems, such as hypertension and an increased risk of heart disease, are common consequences of prolonged exposure to stress hormones.

Moreover, the intricate interplay between the nervous and immune systems highlights the potential impact of anxiety on overall health. Prolonged stress has been linked to immune system suppression, making individuals more susceptible to infections and other illnesses. Recognizing the far-reaching consequences of anxiety on both mind and body emphasizes the need for comprehensive interventions that address psychological and physiological aspects alike.

Common Triggers of Anxiety

Anxiety's triggers, diverse and ubiquitous, underscore its prevalence in our daily lives. Recognizing these triggers empowers individuals to navigate sources of stress, fostering better mental well-being.

1. Stressful Life Events

Life's monumental shifts, from job loss to the loss of a loved one, cast shadows of uncertainty and emotional upheaval, fostering heightened worry and distress.

Navigating the complexities of life requires a delicate balance, and major life events often disrupt this equilibrium. The loss of a job, for example, not only brings financial uncertainties but also challenges one's sense of identity and purpose. Coping with such changes demands resilience and adaptability, qualities that may be compromised in the face of anxiety. Recognizing these events as potential triggers allows individuals to approach them with a heightened awareness and a proactive mindset.

2. Workplace Stress

The demanding pressures of the workplace—tight deadlines, high expectations, and interpersonal conflicts—contribute to work-related anxiety, weaving a tapestry of persistent worry and tension.

The modern workplace, with its fast-paced demands and relentless expectations, has become a breeding ground for anxiety. Meeting tight deadlines, navigating office politics, and striving for professional success can create an environment where stress becomes a constant companion. Understanding the impact of workplace stress on mental health is crucial for individuals and organizations alike. Implementing strategies such as mindfulness programs, flexible work arrangements, and open communication channels can contribute to a healthier work environment.

3. Financial Concerns

The specter of economic instability and financial insecurity unveils a common source of anxiety. Fears of meeting financial obligations echo, creating overwhelming waves of concern.

Financial stability is intricately linked to a sense of security and well-being. The fear of financial instability can cast a long shadow, triggering anxiety, and impacting various aspects of life. Developing financial literacy, creating realistic budgets, and seeking professional advice are valuable tools in navigating the complex landscape of financial anxiety. Moreover, fostering open conversations about money within families and communities reduces the stigma associated with financial challenges, creating a supportive environment for those grappling with anxiety.

4. Social Interactions

Social anxiety transforms everyday interactions into significant triggers, fueled by the fear of judgment, rejection, or embarrassment, leading to avoidance and isolation.

The human need for social connection is profound, making social anxiety a particularly challenging aspect of anxiety disorders. Fear of judgment, rejection, or humiliation in social settings can significantly impede one's ability to form meaningful connections. Encouraging a compassionate understanding of social anxiety, both within oneself and in society, is a crucial step toward dismantling the barriers that isolate individuals. Creating environments that promote inclusivity, understanding, and empathy can be transformative for those navigating the intricate terrain of social anxiety.

5. Health Anxiety

Worries about health, a realm of constant monitoring and catastrophic thinking, echo through health anxiety, creating a landscape of heightened tension.

In an age of readily available health information and increased awareness, concerns about one's health can become a pervasive source of anxiety. The phenomenon known as health anxiety involves excessive worry about having a serious medical condition, often despite reassurance from medical professionals. It is essential to foster health literacy and encourage a balanced perspective on wellness. Promoting self-care practices, regular health check-ups, and destigmatizing discussions about mental health contribute to a more holistic approach to well-being.

6. Uncertainty and Ambiguity

The human quest for predictability collides with anxiety's trigger—uncertainty. Ambiguity, unpredictability, and unknown outcomes unveil vulnerability, fostering discomfort.

The discomfort associated with uncertainty is a universal aspect of the human experience. Anxiety often arises when individuals are faced with ambiguous situations that challenge their sense of control and predictability. Embracing uncertainty as an inherent part of life and developing resilience in the face of unknown outcomes can mitigate anxiety. Mindfulness practices, such as meditation and acceptance-based approaches, offer valuable tools for navigating the discomfort associated with ambiguity.

7. Traumatic Experiences

Trauma, etched in experiences of abuse or violence shapes an individual's journey toward healing, and while we often focus on well-known conditions like PTSD, there's a broader spectrum of experiences. Trauma includes experiences such as combat, abuse, assault, rape, natural disaster, or witnessing these events.

In the aftermath of challenging experiences, individuals understandably navigate a range of emotions, thoughts, and physical responses. Emotional turbulence becomes a part of this journey, with feelings of sadness, guilt, or anger ebbing and flowing. It's like a tapestry of emotions, intricate and unique to each person.

On a cognitive level, the aftermath of trauma can lead to persistent negative beliefs about oneself and the world. Yet, within this complexity, there's room for transformation and reevaluation. It's a process of gently guiding thoughts towards self-compassion and rebuilding trust in the world.

Physically, the body often holds the echoes of trauma, expressing stress in the form of chronic pain, fatigue, or other sensations. The journey toward healing involves acknowledging and addressing these physical manifestations, gradually restoring a sense of safety within one's own body.

Trauma comes in many forms, including day to day experiences that might seem small at first but repeated enough cause Complex PTSD (C-PSTD).

Unlike PTSD, which often stems from a single traumatic incident, C-PTSD unfolds from prolonged exposure to trauma, often involving repeated interpersonal challenges like childhood abuse or neglect. The symptoms of C-PTSD encompass those of PTSD but also include difficulties with emotional regulation, disruptions in self-identity, and challenges in sustaining healthy relationships.

Individuals with C-PTSD may grapple with feelings of emptiness or worthlessness, yet within these struggles lies the potential for profound healing. Nurturing a positive sense of self and navigating interpersonal challenges are essential steps in this transformative journey.

Recognizing and understanding the diverse ways in which trauma may manifest is an empowering approach to supporting individuals on their path to healing. By acknowledging the uniqueness of each person's experience, we can foster a sense of hope, resilience, and the possibility of a brighter future. The journey toward healing is a personal one, filled with opportunities for growth, self-discovery, and the gentle embrace of hope.

Traumatic experiences have a profound impact on mental health, and their aftermath often includes symptoms of anxiety. Recognizing the signs of trauma and providing trauma-informed care are essential steps in supporting individuals on their healing journey. Creating safe spaces for open communication and seeking professional assistance are vital components of addressing the complexities of trauma-related anxiety.

8. Genetic Predisposition

Some carry a genetic legacy predisposing them to anxiety disorders. A familial history becomes a chapter, influencing the likelihood of anxiety symptoms.

The interplay between genetics and anxiety underscores the complex nature of mental health. While genetics can contribute to the predisposition for anxiety disorders, it is crucial to recognize that genetic factors interact with environmental influences. Understanding one's familial history can offer insights into potential risk factors, enabling individuals to make informed choices about their mental health. Moreover, the knowledge of a genetic predisposition emphasizes the importance of early intervention and proactive mental health care.

When to Seek Help

In the embrace of hope, recognizing when to seek help becomes a compass guiding us toward mental well-being. Amidst the ebb and flow of life's emotional tide, certain signposts illuminate the path to professional intervention.

1. Persistent and Intense Symptoms

When anxiety's grip persists, creating prolonged distress and impacting daily life, it may signal the presence of an anxiety disorder—a call to seek professional support.

Persistent and intense symptoms of anxiety can significantly impair an individual's ability to lead a fulfilling and balanced life. Recognizing the duration and intensity of symptoms is crucial in determining the need for professional intervention. Licensed mental health professionals, including psychologists, counselors, and psychiatrists, are equipped to assess and provide appropriate interventions for various anxiety disorders.

2. Impaired Functioning

Anxiety's interference with daily tasks, relationships, or personal goals becomes a poignant indicator, urging individuals to seek help when avoidance behaviors take hold.

Anxiety can exert a powerful influence on various aspects of life, from personal relationships to professional endeavors. Recognizing the impact of anxiety on daily functioning is a key factor in deciding when to seek professional help. Impaired functioning may manifest as difficulties in concentration, disruptions in sleep patterns, or avoidance of activities due to overwhelming anxiety. Seeking assistance during such times is a proactive step toward reclaiming one's ability to lead a meaningful life.

3. Physical Health Issues

The toll of chronic anxiety on physical health manifested through cardiovascular issues or gastrointestinal disorders, signals a crucial need for healthcare intervention.

The intricate connection between mental and physical health emphasizes the importance of addressing both aspects in anxiety management. Chronic anxiety can contribute to a range of physical health issues, including cardiovascular problems and gastrointestinal disorders. Seeking the guidance of healthcare professionals ensures a comprehensive approach to well-being, addressing both the psychological and physiological dimensions of anxiety.

4. Self-Harm or Suicidal Thoughts:

Any whispers of self-harm or thoughts of suicide demand immediate attention, an urgent call to reach out to mental health professionals or emergency services.

The presence of self-harm or suicidal thoughts requires urgent and compassionate intervention. Individuals experiencing such thoughts should seek immediate assistance from mental health professionals, helplines, or emergency services. The complexity of these experiences necessitates specialized care, and a supportive network of mental health professionals can provide the necessary interventions to ensure safety and recovery.

5. Interference with Relationships

Anxiety's strain on relationships calls for therapeutic exploration, offering insights and strategies to mend interpersonal dynamics.

The impact of anxiety extends beyond the individual, influencing interpersonal relationships and dynamics. Strained relationships can further exacerbate feelings of isolation and distress. Seeking therapeutic exploration provides a supportive space to understand and address the impact of anxiety on relationships. Relationship-focused interventions, such as couples counseling or family therapy, offer valuable tools for rebuilding connections and fostering a supportive environment.

6. Inability to Cope:

When the tools for coping with anxiety prove insufficient, seeking the guidance of a mental health professional becomes a beacon of resilience.

Coping mechanisms are essential in managing anxiety, but there are instances when individuals find their usual strategies inadequate. Seeking the guidance of mental health professionals introduces new coping strategies tailored to the individual's unique needs. Professional support provides an opportunity to explore and develop effective coping mechanisms that promote resilience and well-being.

7. Recurrent Panic Attacks

The recurrence of panic attacks, with their intense physical and psychological manifestations, beckons individuals toward seeking professional help, unlocking pathways to prevention and management.

Panic attacks can be distressing and debilitating, often accompanied by intense physical sensations and overwhelming fear. Recurrent panic attacks may indicate an underlying anxiety disorder that requires professional attention. Seeking help during the early stages of recurrent panic attacks allows for timely intervention, preventing further escalation and promoting effective management strategies.

Anxiety is a rich tapestry of human experience—a complex blend of psychology and physiology, woven with diverse triggers. While mild anxiety whispers through the fabric of our lives, persistent and severe symptoms invite us to embrace the prospect of professional help without stigma. Through therapy, medication, or a harmonious blend of both, avenues of exploration open up on the journey toward mental well-being.

May the understanding of anxiety be a source of compassion and illumination—a testament to the resilience within us all. In the canvas of our emotions, anxiety paints shades of challenge and opportunity. Let us, with hope as our guide, tread these paths with courage, seeking support when needed, and finding solace in the shared journey toward lasting well-being. The journey toward understanding anxiety is not merely an exploration of its challenges but an invitation to discover the strength, resilience, and transformative potential within. As we unravel the intricate threads of anxiety, may we find the threads of hope, compassion, and healing intertwined, guiding us toward a future of serenity and well-being.

Anxiety and the Mind-Body Connection

In the intricate dance of emotions, anxiety emerges as a prevalent and intricate thread that binds the mind and body in a profound embrace. This exploration ventures into the depths of the mind-body connection, unraveling the complex ways anxiety influences both our psychological experiences and physiological responses. We also illuminate the path of healing from anxiety, emphasizing the psychological dimensions of natural remedies and the significance of adopting a holistic approach for enduring well-being.

The Mind-Body Connection

Within the human experience, the mind and body form a harmonious, bidirectional relationship, each influencing and responding to the other. This profound connection is fundamental to our understanding of anxiety's impact on mental and physical well-being.

Neurotransmitters and Hormones:

Anxiety, as a maestro of emotions, orchestrates the brain's neurotransmitter symphony and hormonal balance. Serotonin, dopamine, and norepinephrine, the conductors of mood and stress responses, find their cadence disrupted in various anxiety disorders. The stress-induced release of cortisol, the famed stress hormone, takes center stage, influencing physical symptoms like increased heart rate and disrupted sleep patterns.

This disruption in neurotransmitters and hormones highlights the intricate interplay between psychological and physiological factors in anxiety. Understanding these chemical messengers provides a foundation for exploring interventions that target specific pathways, offering potential relief to those navigating the complexities of anxiety.

Impact on the Immune System:

The melody of prolonged stress and anxiety can echo through the immune system, compromising its resilience. Cortisol, the conductor of this symphony, may lead to inflammation, rendering individuals more susceptible to illnesses and impairing their ability to recover.

The immune system's response to stress underscores the intricate connection between mental and physical health. Chronic stress, often accompanied by anxiety, can weaken the immune system, making the body more susceptible to infections and diseases. This revelation emphasizes the importance of holistic approaches that address both psychological and physiological aspects of well-being.

Cardiovascular Effects:

Anxiety's resonance extends to the cardiovascular system, weaving a heightened state of arousal and an increased heart rate into its rhythm. Chronic anxiety, the persistent melody, has been linked to cardiovascular risks, inviting hypertension and atherosclerosis into the composition.

The cardiovascular impact of anxiety is a stark reminder of the far-reaching consequences of prolonged stress. Individuals grappling with anxiety may face an increased risk of heart-related issues. Integrative interventions that promote relaxation and cardiovascular health become essential components in the comprehensive approach to anxiety management.

Musculoskeletal Impact:

The body, a canvas of responses, echoes anxiety through muscle tension. In its instinctive response to stress, muscles contract, creating a symphony of stiffness, aches, and chronic pain. Conditions like tension headaches and temporomandibular joint (TMJ) dysfunction dance in cadence with persistent muscle tension caused by anxiety.

Musculoskeletal manifestations of anxiety highlight the intricate connection between mental and physical tension. Recognizing the impact on muscles and joints opens avenues for interventions such as relaxation techniques, physical therapy, and body-mind practices that release muscular tension.

Respiratory System Effects:

Anxiety, the unseen conductor, directs breathing patterns, orchestrating hyperventilation, or shallow breaths. The result is a symphony of dizziness, chest tightness, and shortness of breath. Chronic anxiety may contribute to respiratory issues, amplifying conditions like asthma.

The respiratory effects of anxiety emphasize the importance of breath awareness and respiratory interventions in anxiety management. Techniques that promote diaphragmatic breathing and mindfulness contribute to regulating respiratory patterns, offering relief to individuals experiencing the breath-related symptoms of anxiety.

Gastrointestinal Consequences:

The gut-brain axis, a duet of interconnectedness, reveals anxiety's influence on the gastrointestinal tract. Nausea, stomachaches, and changes in bowel habits perform a delicate dance. Conditions like irritable bowel syndrome (IBS) intricately intertwine with the stress and anxiety narrative.

Gastrointestinal consequences of anxiety illuminate the intricate interplay between the gut and the brain. Dietary interventions, gut-health-focused strategies, and stress-reduction techniques become essential elements in the holistic approach to anxiety relief, acknowledging the significance of the gut-brain connection.

Nourishing the Mind

Now that you understand the different types of anxiety, the many reasons behind anxiety, and when anxiety is beyond the scope of this book, let's focus on healing. The next chapters will lead you to foods that will help with anxiety, ways to connect with nature and herbs, physical movement as healing, meditation, and mindfulness. Explore these healing ideas, then in the last chapter, we will work to put together a personalized map of anxiety curatives to use as a daily practice toward health.

In the vibrant realm of well-being, the relationship between diet and mental health emerges as a blossoming field of discovery. As our understanding deepens, it becomes increasingly clear that the foods we choose play a vital role in shaping our mental landscape, particularly in the realm of anxiety. In this exploration, we embark on a journey through dietary adjustments designed to tenderly combat anxiety. Our path will wind through foods known to be allies in the battle against anxiety symptoms, gently avoiding those that may heighten unease. Along the way, we'll pause to appreciate herbal supplements and vitamins that lend their support to the body's resilience in the face of stress.

Foods that Bring Comfort

1. Fatty Fish:

Let's cast our net into the soothing waters of fatty fish—salmon, mackerel, and sardines. Rich in omega-3 fatty acids, these treasures from the sea are revered for their brain-boosting prowess. By regulating neurotransmitters and reducing brain inflammation, these omega-3s create a melody of mental well-being, lowering the risk of anxiety and depression. Work to incorporate fatty fish into your meals at least 2 times per week.

2. Whole Grains:

Picture the comforting embrace of whole grains—brown rice, quinoa, and oats. These complex carbohydrates are our steadfast companions, maintaining stable blood sugar levels. In this stability, we find a haven for anxiety management. Whole grains, rich in serotonin-boosting nutrients, become pillars of well-being. Whole grains can be eaten daily.

3. Leafy Greens:

Venture into the lush garden of leafy greens—spinach and kale standing tall. Here, we discover magnesium, a mineral that orchestrates the body's stress response. With leafy greens, we cultivate resilience against anxiety, ensuring our magnesium levels dance in harmony with our well-being. Leafy greens should be incorporated into most meals.

Not interested in kale for breakfast? Try it in a nourishing green smoothie! The following recipe incorporates many of the foods mentioned here:

Ingredients:

- 1 cup fresh spinach leaves, washed

- 1 cup kale leaves, stems removed and chopped

- 1 banana, peeled and sliced

- 1/2 cucumber, peeled and sliced

- 1/2 green apple, cored and chopped

- 1/2 lemon, juiced

- 1 cup coconut water or water

- 1/2 cup ice cubes (optional)

- 1 tablespoon chia seeds or flaxseeds (optional, for added nutrition)

Instructions:

1. Prepare the Ingredients: Wash the spinach and kale thoroughly. Peel and slice the banana and cucumber. Core and chop the green apple. Juice the lemon.

2. Combine Ingredients: In a blender, add the fresh spinach, chopped kale, banana slices, cucumber slices, chopped green apple, and the juice of half a lemon.

3. Add Liquid: Pour in the coconut water or water.

4. Optional Additions: If you like, add ice cubes for a colder and refreshing smoothie. You can also include chia seeds or flaxseeds for added fiber and nutrients.

5. Blend: Blend all the ingredients until you achieve a smooth and creamy consistency. If the smoothie is too thick, you can add more liquid.

6. Serve: Pour the green smoothie into a glass and enjoy immediately! Feel free to garnish with additional chia seeds or a slice of lemon if desired.

This green smoothie is not only delicious but also packed with anxiety-reducing ingredients. Adjust the quantities to suit your taste preferences, and feel free to experiment with additional fruits or vegetables to personalize your green smoothie experience.

4. Probiotics and Fermented Foods:

A journey into the intricate dance of the gut-brain connection reveals probiotics in yogurt, kefir, and sauerkraut. These probiotics, like skilled choreographers, bring balance to our gut bacteria. A harmonious gut microbiome, we learn, fosters improved mood and lessens the grip of anxiety.

5. Nuts and Seeds:

As we crack open the treasures of almonds, walnuts, and chia seeds, we uncover nutrients that champion brain health. Omega-3 fatty acids, magnesium, and zinc found within these treasures compose a symphony that regulates neurotransmitters, offering relief to those seeking respite from anxiety.

6. Turmeric:

In the vibrant hues of turmeric, we find curcumin—an ally against inflammation and oxidative stress. This golden compound stands as a beacon, guiding us away from anxiety's shadows. A sip of turmeric becomes a soothing elixir, calming the storm within.

7. Dark Chocolate:

Indulge, but with mindfulness, in the decadence of dark chocolate. Rich in flavonoids, this treat boasts antioxidant properties that weave a tapestry of stress reduction. In moderation, it whispers a sweet promise of mood enhancement and gentle energy—a momentary respite from anxiety's grip.

8. Bananas:

In the orchards, bananas sway, offering potassium—a balm for blood pressure regulation. A stable rhythm is found in the daily intake of these potassium-rich delights, nurturing equilibrium. Within, vitamin B6 joins the chorus, playing a role in the production of serotonin, our ally in the journey to tranquility.

There are many foods that work with our body to help heal anxiety and the physiologic effects of anxiety. However, there are also foods that can increase anxiety and its effects upon the body.

Foods to Tread Lightly On

1. Caffeine:

The morning ritual of coffee brings warmth, but tread lightly, for excessive caffeine may stir restlessness. A stimulant, it quickens the heartbeat and can disturb the peace of sleep—a cautionary note in the symphony of anxiety management.

2. Refined Sugar:

The sweet melody of sugar can turn sour when fluctuations in blood sugar disrupt our mood. Opt for the steady cadence of complex carbohydrates, as refined sugars may contribute to irritability and unrest—a gentle pivot toward stability.

There are many complex carbohydrate substitutes for refined sugar. Experiment with several, as each will complement foods in different ways.

- Honey is a natural sweetener that contains complex carbohydrates along with various vitamins and minerals. It also has antioxidant and antimicrobial properties.

- Maple syrup is a natural sweetener made from the sap of maple trees. It contains complex carbohydrates, as well as some minerals like manganese and zinc.

- Agave nectar is derived from the agave plant and is a lower glycemic index sweetener compared to refined sugar. It is a source of complex carbohydrates.

- Date sugar is made from dried, ground dates. It contains fiber and other nutrients, making it a good complex carbohydrate alternative to refined sugar.

- Coconut sugar is made from the sap of coconut palm trees. It contains small amounts of nutrients like iron, zinc, and antioxidants, providing a more complex carbohydrate profile.

- Molasses, especially blackstrap molasses, is a byproduct of the sugar refining process and contains significant amounts of vitamins and minerals, such as iron and calcium.

- Using natural fruit purees like applesauce, mashed bananas, or pureed dates can add natural sweetness and complex carbohydrates to recipes.

- Stevia is a natural sweetener derived from the leaves of the Stevia rebaudiana plant. While it is intensely sweet and low in calories, it does not contribute carbohydrates. Consider combining it with other complex carbohydrate sources for balance.

- Barley malt syrup is a natural sweetener made from malted barley. It contains complex carbohydrates and has a rich, malty flavor.

- Brown rice syrup is made from fermented brown rice and contains complex carbohydrates. It is less sweet than some other alternatives but provides a subtle sweetness.

3. Alcohol:

In the quietude of a glass, some seek solace. Yet, alcohol, a silent depressant, may disrupt our dreams. It casts shadows on mood and energy, reminding us to approach it with mindfulness, aware of its potential impact on our mental landscape.

4. Processed Foods:

The allure of processed foods, with their artificial additives and preservatives, masks a potential toll on mental well-being. These culinary illusions, stripped of essential nutrients, may compromise our resilience against stress and amplify vulnerability to anxiety.

5. High-Sodium Foods:

In the world of flavors, high-sodium delights may tempt, but caution is our guide. For elevated blood pressure, a consequence of high sodium, may echo in feelings of tension and unease—a reminder to choose with a heart mindful of cardiovascular health.

6. Trans Fats:

The sizzle of frying pans conjures visions of trans fats—an offering found in processed and fried foods. These fats, harbingers of inflammation, cast shadows on neurotransmitter function, linking arms with anxiety. A mindful step away becomes an act of self-care.

7. Artificial Sweeteners:

In the pursuit of sweetness, artificial companions beckon. While the connection awaits further understanding, those with anxiety may choose to limit these sweet whispers—a gentle pause, allowing space for well-being.

It can be difficult in our busy world to craft a menu of perfectly balanced nutrition. Consider the following supplements as you walk the journey toward healing anxiety. Speaking with a nutritionist will help you find the best supportive supplements that will help your anxiety symptoms.

Supplements for Gentle Support

1. Omega-3 Fatty Acids:

The bounty of the sea finds its way into supplements, encapsulating the wisdom of omega-3 fatty acids. In the form of fish oil supplements, EPA and DHA extend a hand, offering potential benefits in the easing of anxiety symptoms—a gentle ally in the journey to tranquility.

2. Magnesium:

The embrace of magnesium extends beyond foods to supplements, particularly for those with deficiencies. A crucial conductor in neurotransmitter regulation, magnesium supplements harmonize with the body's stress response. In this harmony, we discover another avenue for anxiety support.

3. Probiotics:

As guardians of gut health, probiotic supplements beckon. Their dance in the symphony of a balanced microbiome may hold promise for mental well-being. A daily note in the supplement regimen, offering a holistic approach to anxiety management.

4. Lavender Oil:

In the aromatic realm, lavender oil unfolds its petals. Inhaled or applied, its calming properties may cradle moments of respite from anxiety. A gentle whisper in the breeze, offers a fragrant pathway to tranquility.

5. Valerian Root:

From the herbal haven, valerian root emerges—a traditional remedy for anxiety and sleep disorders. Its interaction with GABA receptors evokes a sense of calm. A botanical ally, its use invites consultation with healthcare providers—a mindful step in the quest for serenity.

6. Vitamin B Complex:

In the pantheon of B vitamins, the complex emerges—a guardian of neurotransmitter synthesis and brain health. As a supplement, it extends a hand, supporting the body's resilience to stress. A nutrient-rich note in the symphony of anxiety management.

7. Ashwagandha:

From the roots of adaptogenic wisdom, ashwagandha stands tall—a stress-relieving companion. Its gentle touch aids the body in adapting to stress, fostering calm. Yet, with any herbal supplement, a conversation with healthcare professionals becomes a guiding compass—an informed step toward well-being.

8. L-Theanine:

In the green embrace of tea leaves, L-Theanine whispers serenity. In supplement form, its non-drowsy calming effects offer a gentle balm. A companion in the pursuit of tranquility, it finds its place in the comprehensive plan for anxiety management.

Let us reflect on the symphony of nourishment that accompanies the journey to anxiety relief. Dietary adjustments, like gentle refrains, play a significant role in our multifaceted approach to well-being. Each choice—whether a comforting food, a cautious step around triggers, or a supplement extending support—is a note in the composition of our mental landscape.

It is with kindness towards ourselves that we approach these adjustments, recognizing their place within a broader tapestry of well-being. In concert with therapy, medication as advised by healthcare professionals, and evidence-based interventions, dietary choices weave together to enhance the effectiveness of our anxiety management strategies.

In the sanctuary of balanced and nutrient-rich choices, we find an ally—a reminder that our well-being is a harmonious dance between physical and mental realms. As we tread this path with mindfulness, may each bite, each sip, and each supplement becomes a gentle reminder of our commitment to serenity—a commitment to the vibrant, resilient symphony of well-being.

Exploring the Nuances of Anxiety and Diet

As we delve further into the intricate relationship between diet and anxiety relief, it becomes essential to acknowledge the nuanced nature of anxiety itself. Anxiety is not a monolithic experience but a complex interplay of genetic, environmental, and psychological factors. Understanding this complexity is crucial as we navigate the landscape of dietary adjustments. Different individuals may respond uniquely to dietary changes, making it imperative to approach this exploration with a personalized perspective.

The Gut-Brain Axis

A captivating aspect of the mind-diet connection is the gut-brain axis as discussed earlier. This bidirectional communication highway reveals the profound impact of our gut health on mental well-being. Emerging research continues to illuminate the intricate dialogue between the gut and the brain, highlighting the role of the gut microbiome in influencing mood and cognition.

Probiotics, the beneficial bacteria found in fermented foods and supplements, play a pivotal role in maintaining a healthy gut microbiome. These microbial allies contribute not only to digestive health but also to the production of neurotransmitters like serotonin, often referred to as the "feel-good" neurotransmitter. The inclusion of probiotics in our dietary repertoire becomes a strategic move in supporting both digestive and mental health.

Mindful Eating Practices

Beyond the specific foods we consume, the way we eat also holds significance in the realm of anxiety relief. Mindful eating practices invite us to cultivate a heightened awareness of our eating habits, fostering a deeper connection between mind and body. By savoring each bite, chewing slowly, and paying attention to the sensory experience of eating, we invite a sense of calm into our meals.

Moreover, let's delve into an exercise that can be incorporated into mindful eating, enhancing its therapeutic benefits. One impactful practice is the "Five Senses Eating Meditation." This exercise involves bringing mindful attention to each of the five senses during a meal:

1. Sight: Take a moment to visually appreciate the colors, textures, and arrangement of your food. Notice the vibrant hues, the play of light and shadow, and the overall presentation. Allow your eyes to savor the aesthetic richness before you.

2. Touch: Engage your sense of touch by noticing the temperature and texture of your food. Feel the warmth or coolness against your fingertips. Be aware of the varying textures as you explore different components of your meal.

3. Smell: Bring your attention to the aromas rising from your plate. Inhale deeply and appreciate the diverse scents. Take a moment to identify the individual ingredients and let the fragrances contribute to the anticipation of the upcoming flavors.

4. Hearing: While eating, listen to the sounds associated with your meal. This could include the gentle sizzle of cooking, the crunch of fresh vegetables, or the soft hum of your surroundings. Allow these sounds to ground you in the present moment.

5. Taste: Finally, savor each bite intentionally. Pay attention to the flavors as they unfold on your palate. Notice the subtle nuances and the way different ingredients complement each other. Take your time to experience the full spectrum of tastes.

Practicing mindfulness during meals also includes being attuned to hunger and fullness cues. Understanding the signals our body sends can guide us in making nourishing choices that align with our individual needs. Mindful eating is not only about what is on the plate but also about the experience of eating, creating a holistic approach to well-being.

By incorporating mindful eating exercises like the Five Senses Eating Meditation into our routine, we deepen our connection with the present moment, fostering a harmonious relationship with food. This practice extends beyond the act of nourishment, becoming a mindful and intentional celebration of the sensory richness that each meal brings. As we cultivate this awareness, we contribute to the holistic well-being of both body and mind, inviting tranquility into our daily nourishment rituals.

Harnessing the Power of Adaptogens

While we've touched upon the herbal ally, ashwagandha, it's essential to explore the broader category of adaptogens concerning anxiety relief. Adaptogens are a class of herbs known for their ability to help the body adapt to stress and restore balance. Ginseng, rhodiola, and holy basil are among the adaptogens that have been studied for their potential benefits in managing stress and anxiety.

These herbs often come in supplement form or can be incorporated into teas and tinctures. Ginseng, for instance, has been linked to improved mood and reduced fatigue, while holy basil is revered for its calming properties. As with any supplementation, consulting with healthcare professionals ensures a safe and personalized approach to incorporating adaptogens into one's anxiety management strategy. Chapter Four will delve deeper into herbs for anxiety relief.

The Intersection of Diet and Lifestyle:

A holistic approach to anxiety relief involves recognizing the interconnectedness of diet and lifestyle factors. Regular physical activity, adequate sleep, and stress management techniques complement dietary adjustments, forming a robust foundation for overall well-being.

Exercise, a powerful antidote to stress, not only enhances mood through the release of endorphins but also contributes to improved sleep quality. Quality sleep, in turn, supports cognitive function and emotional resilience. The intricate dance between lifestyle elements and dietary choices creates a harmonious symphony, each element reinforcing the other in the quest for anxiety relief. Chapter Five will discuss ways to incorporate exercise for anxiety healing into your daily life.

Navigating Dietary Restrictions:

It's essential to acknowledge that individual dietary needs vary, and some individuals may navigate anxiety within the context of specific dietary restrictions or preferences. Vegan, vegetarian, gluten-free, or other dietary patterns require thoughtful consideration to ensure a balanced intake of essential nutrients.

For those with dietary restrictions, a tailored approach involves identifying alternative sources for key nutrients typically found in animal products or gluten-containing foods. This may include consulting with a nutritionist or dietitian to craft a well-rounded eating plan that meets both nutritional and anxiety management needs.

Culinary Creativity and Joy:

Amidst the strategic considerations of anxiety-focused dietary adjustments, it's crucial not to lose sight of the joy and creativity that food can bring into our lives. Exploring new recipes, savoring diverse flavors, and sharing meals with loved ones contribute not only to our physical health but also to the emotional tapestry of well-being.

Culinary creativity becomes a form of self-expression and self-care. Engaging in the art of cooking allows individuals to connect with the process of nourishment on a deeper level, transforming meals into moments of mindfulness and delight. The intersection of joy and nutrition becomes a cornerstone in the construction of a resilient and balanced mind.

We encourage you to have fun while exploring the different food choices here. Nourishing meals for oneself and loved ones become joyful expressions of community and love.

Cultivating Sustainable Habits:

As we weave together the threads of dietary adjustments for anxiety relief, it's crucial to emphasize the sustainability of these habits. Establishing a sustainable and realistic approach to dietary changes ensures that they become integral components of one's lifestyle rather than fleeting endeavors.

Sustainability encompasses not only the practicality of dietary choices but also their psychological and emotional resonance. Fostering a positive relationship with food involves embracing flexibility, allowing for occasional indulgences, and approaching dietary adjustments with self-compassion. The goal is not perfection but rather a sustainable and nourishing journey towards enhanced well-being.

In the expansive landscape of dietary adjustments for anxiety relief, we uncover a rich tapestry of interconnected elements. From the influence of the gut microbiome to the mindful practice of eating and the inclusion of adaptogens, each facet contributes to a continuum of nourishment for the mind.

By embracing the personalized and multifaceted nature of anxiety, individuals can craft a dietary symphony that resonates with their unique needs and preferences. The goal is not a rigid set of rules but a fluid and evolving exploration of the relationship between what we consume and how we feel.

As we navigate this continuum of nourishment, let us approach each meal, each choice, and each adjustment with a spirit of curiosity, self-compassion, and a commitment to fostering a resilient and harmonious mind. In this dynamic interplay of dietary elements, may individuals find not only relief from anxiety but also a celebration of the vibrant and interconnected journey toward well-being.

Embracing Serenity

Embarking on a journey through time, herbal remedies unfold as cherished allies in the pursuit of tranquility and well-being. For centuries, these gentle emissaries from nature have whispered soothing secrets to those seeking calmness in the midst of life's storms. In this enchanting exploration, we unravel a tapestry of herbs celebrated for their calming dance—offering a comforting and holistic way to gracefully navigate the currents of stress and anxiety. Join us as we introduce these herbal maestros, guiding you through the art of crafting teas, tinctures, and elixirs while embracing the importance of safety and understanding the nuanced language of herb interactions.

Herbs for a Gentle Embrace

As we embark on an extended exploration of nature's herbal elixirs, let us dive deeper into the individual virtues of these time-honored remedies. Each herb, with its unique properties and characteristics, contributes to the symphony of tranquility in its own distinct way.

Chamomile (Matricaria chamomilla):

Chamomile, with its delicate golden blooms, has long been revered for its calming effects. The compound apigenin, found in chamomile, engages with receptors in the brain to induce relaxation and mitigate anxiety. Beyond its psychological benefits, chamomile is also renowned for its digestive properties. Crafting a chamomile tea involves infusing dried chamomile flowers in hot water, allowing the essence of serenity to bloom in every cup.

Expanding on the art of chamomile tea, consider incorporating it into bedtime rituals. The ritual of sipping chamomile tea before sleep becomes a gentle signal to the body and mind, preparing them for a restful night's sleep. The quiet moments of reflection while sipping this herbal elixir contribute to a holistic approach to managing stress and anxiety.

Lavender (Lavandula angustifolia):

Lavender, with its enchanting fragrance, transcends its ornamental use and emerges as a powerful herbal ally in the pursuit of serenity. The essential oil derived from lavender is a versatile elixir that finds its way into various forms of herbal craft, from teas to tinctures.

In the realm of aromatherapy, lavender takes center stage. Consider the art of infusing lavender essential oil into diffusers or incorporating it into soothing baths. The aromatic tendrils of lavender oil gently caress the senses, inducing a state of calmness and relaxation. The practice of incorporating lavender into self-care routines, such as through lavender-scented bath salts or pillows, adds a touch of tranquility to everyday life.

Valerian (Valeriana officinalis):

Valerian, with its ancient reputation as a calming herb, is celebrated for its sedative properties. The compounds within valerian interact with GABA receptors in the brain, contributing to a sense of calmness and aiding in the management of anxiety. While its distinct aroma may not be everyone's preference, valerian's efficacy as a natural sedative is well-established.

To further explore the benefits of valerian, delve into the world of herbal tinctures. Crafting a valerian tincture involves steeping the dried root of the valerian plant in alcohol or glycerin, allowing its calming essence to be extracted. This tincture can be conveniently added to beverages, offering a measured dose of tranquility.

Passionflower (Passiflora incarnata):

Passionflower, adorned with intricate blooms, has earned its place among herbal remedies for anxiety and insomnia. The plant's anxiolytic properties are attributed to its ability to increase GABA levels in the brain, inducing a calming effect. Exploring passionflower in various herbal forms allows for a nuanced understanding of its calming virtues.

Crafting a herbal blend that combines passionflower with other calming herbs, such as chamomile or lemon balm, amplifies the overall calming effect. In the world of herbal teas, the fusion of passionflower with complimentary herbs creates a symphony of soothing notes that resonate through each sip.

Lemon Balm (Melissa officinalis):

Lemon balm, a member of the mint family, contributes to the herbal arsenal for managing stress and anxiety. Its compounds engage with GABA receptors, promoting a gentle uplift in mood and overall well-being. Incorporating lemon balm into herbal crafts, especially teas, reveals its citrusy brightness and soothing properties.

Consider exploring the art of blending lemon balm with other herbs known for their calming effects. An herbal tea blend that marries lemon balm with lavender or chamomile creates a delightful infusion that appeals to the senses while offering a respite from the demands of daily life.

Ashwagandha (Withania somnifera):

Ashwagandha, rooted in the ancient wisdom of Ayurveda, emerges as an adaptogenic ally in the battle against stress. Its unique ability to modulate the stress response and balance hormones makes it a valuable herbal remedy. While it is commonly available in supplement form, exploring its powdered form allows for versatile integration into daily wellness routines.

Crafting an ashwagandha-infused golden milk offers a delicious and nourishing way to experience the herb's benefits. Combining ashwagandha with other warming spices like turmeric, ginger, and cinnamon creates a wholesome elixir that not only promotes relaxation but also supports overall health.

Experiment with this recipe for Ashwagandha-Infused Golden Milk, also known as "golden latte".

Ingredients:

- 1 cup unsweetened almond milk (or any plant-based milk of your choice)

- 1/2 teaspoon ground turmeric

- 1/4 teaspoon ground cinnamon

- 1/8 teaspoon ground ginger (or freshly grated ginger)

- 1/8 teaspoon ground black pepper

- 1/2 to 1 teaspoon ashwagandha powder (adjust to your preference)

- 1-2 teaspoons honey or maple syrup (optional, for sweetness)

- 1/2 teaspoon coconut oil (optional, for richness)

- A dash of vanilla extract (optional, for flavor)

Instructions:

1. Heat the Milk: In a small saucepan, gently heat the almond milk over medium heat. Be careful not to bring it to a boil; you just want it warm.

2. Mix in the Spices: Add the turmeric, cinnamon, ginger, and black pepper to the warm milk. Whisk the mixture well to ensure that the spices are evenly distributed.

3. Add Ashwagandha: Stir in the ashwagandha powder, adjusting the quantity based on your preference for taste and desired effect.

4. Sweeten to Taste: If desired, add honey or maple syrup to sweeten the golden milk. Start with a small amount and adjust according to your sweetness preference.

5. Enhance with Optional Ingredients: For added richness, you can include coconut oil and a dash of vanilla extract. Stir well to incorporate these optional ingredients.

6. Simmer and Strain (Optional): Allow the golden milk to simmer for a few minutes, but do not let it boil. This step is optional, but it can help infuse the flavors. If you've used fresh ginger, you may want to strain the milk before serving.

7. Serve: Pour the ashwagandha-infused golden milk into your favorite mug and enjoy the comforting, soothing flavors.

It's a wonderful beverage to incorporate into your evening routine for relaxation and stress relief. Adjust the ingredients to suit your taste preferences and individual needs.

Rhodiola (Rhodiola rosea):

Rhodiola, another notable adaptogen, thrives in harsh climates and has adapted to offer resilience against stress. Its benefits extend beyond psychological well-being to include physical endurance and cognitive support. Considering rhodiola in supplement form allows for precise and controlled doses.

Delving into the research on rhodiola unveils its potential to enhance cognitive function. Crafting a ritual around incorporating rhodiola supplements into morning routines aligns with its adaptogenic nature, fostering a sense of balance and fortitude as one faces the challenges of the day.

Kava Kava (Piper methysticum):

Originating from the South Pacific, kava kava presents a unique herbal elixir with sedative properties. Traditionally consumed as a ceremonial beverage, kava kava induces relaxation and tranquility. Exploring kava kava in various forms, such as teas, capsules, or tinctures, allows for a personalized approach to herbal wellness.

To elevate the experience of consuming kava kava, consider exploring the traditional preparation method. Brewing kava kava in a ceremonial fashion involves kneading the root in water and extracting its soothing compounds. This ritualistic approach adds a cultural dimension to the consumption of kava kava, fostering a connection with its historical use.

It's important to note that the effects of kava can vary, and individual reactions may differ. If you're considering trying kava, it's recommended to choose noble kava varieties and consult with a healthcare professional, especially if you have liver issues or are taking medications. Additionally, be mindful of local regulations, as kava consumption is restricted or banned in some regions.

Herbal Crafting as a Ritual of Self-Care

In the expanded exploration of herbal remedies, it becomes evident that crafting herbal elixirs is not merely a utilitarian act but a ritual of self-care. The process of selecting, preparing, and consuming herbs transforms into a mindful journey that aligns with the principles of holistic wellness.

Herbal Teas:

The act of brewing herbal teas evolves into a meditative practice. As the herbs steep in hot water, their essence mingles with the steam, creating an aromatic symphony. Let's infuse this ritual with the soothing qualities of chamomile by incorporating a simple recipe for calming chamomile tea.

Calming Chamomile Tea Recipe:

Ingredients:

- 1 tablespoon dried chamomile flowers

- 1 cup hot water

- Optional: Honey or lemon for flavor

Instructions:

1. Begin by bringing a cup of water to a gentle boil.

2. Place the dried chamomile flowers in a teapot or a heat-proof container.

3. Pour the hot water over the chamomile flowers.

4. Let the tea steep for about 5 minutes, allowing the chamomile to release its calming properties.

5. Strain the tea to remove the chamomile flowers.

6. Optional: Add honey or a squeeze of lemon for extra flavor.

Consider dedicating a specific time each day to the preparation and enjoyment of this chamomile tea. This ritualistic approach transforms the act of tea-drinking into a deliberate pause—a moment of reflection and relaxation amidst the busyness of life. Creating a designated tea corner, adorned with dried herbs, infusers, and beautiful teacups, enhances the visual and sensory aspects of the ritual.

As you sip on your chamomile tea, let the warm liquid and the gentle aroma transport you to a tranquil state of mind. This intentional mindfulness during tea preparation becomes an opportunity to foster a deeper connection with the calming virtues of nature, offering a peaceful interlude in your day.

Tinctures:

Crafting herbal tinctures unfolds as an alchemical endeavor—an intimate dance with the essence of plants. The process of allowing herbs to macerate in alcohol or glycerin becomes a form of herbal extraction that mirrors the slow passage of time. Engaging in tincture crafting as a ritual invites a sense of patience and connection with the gradual unfolding of nature's wisdom.

In the realm of herbal tinctures, consider the gentle yet potent lemon balm. To incorporate this soothing herb into your wellness repertoire, you can create a homemade lemon balm tincture. Begin by selecting high-quality dried lemon balm leaves. Place these leaves in a clean glass jar, ensuring they fill about one-third of the container.

Next, choose a menstruum that aligns with your preferences. Traditional tinctures often use alcohol, like vodka or brandy, for its excellent extracting properties. For a glycerin-based tincture, select food-grade glycerin. Pour the chosen menstruum over the lemon balm leaves, covering them completely.

Seal the jar tightly and place it in a cool, dark location. Allow the lemon balm to macerate for at least 4-6 weeks, shaking the jar gently every few days to encourage the herbal infusion. As the weeks pass, you'll witness the transformation—the liquid taking on the vibrant green hue of lemon balm's essence.

When the maceration period is complete, strain the tincture using a fine mesh strainer or cheesecloth, separating the liquid from the spent herbs. Collect the potent liquid in a clean, dark glass bottle, marking the culmination of this alchemical process.

Establishing a tincture crafting ritual involves not only the technical aspects but also an intention to connect with the plants' healing energy. As you bottle the lemon balm tincture, infuse the process with gratitude for the plant's wisdom and a sense of anticipation for the well-being it will soon offer.

Now, your homemade lemon balm tincture becomes a personalized herbal remedy, a treasure to be incorporated into daily wellness practices. A few drops under the tongue, added to a calming tea, or blended into your favorite wellness elixir—this tincture carries the essence of lemon balm's calming properties, offering a soothing balm for both body and spirit.

Herbal Capsules:

The convenience of herbal capsules does not diminish the ritualistic aspect of incorporating herbs into one's wellness routine. The act of taking herbal capsules becomes a deliberate choice—a commitment to self-care. Creating a ritual around capsule consumption involves setting aside a few moments each day for this intentional practice.

Consider infusing this ritual with mindfulness by taking a moment to reflect on the specific benefits of each herb contained in the capsules. This reflective pause transforms the act of swallowing capsules into a conscious acknowledgment of the therapeutic journey they represent. Creating a dedicated space for herbal capsules, perhaps alongside other wellness items, emphasizes their significance in the broader tapestry of self-care.

Aromatherapy:

Inhaling the fragrant essence of herbal aromas transcends the functional act of diffusing essential oils. Aromatherapy becomes a sensory journey—a ritual that engages both the olfactory and limbic systems. The act of choosing specific essential oils and creating aromatic blends adds a creative dimension to this ritual of self-care.

Establishing an aromatherapy ritual involves selecting essential oils based on their therapeutic properties. Crafting blends that cater to specific moods or needs enhances the personalized nature of this ritual. Diffusing essential oils during moments of relaxation, such as during meditation or before bedtime, amplifies their calming effects, creating a fragrant sanctuary of tranquility.

Herbal Baths:

Immersing oneself in a herbal bath unfolds as a luxurious and therapeutic ritual of self-care. The act of preparing an herbal bath involves selecting dried herbs or essential oils that contribute to relaxation and stress relief. Let's enhance this experience with the calming aroma of lavender, known for its soothing properties.

Begin by gathering a handful of dried lavender flowers or a few drops of lavender essential oil. If using dried lavender, consider placing it in a porous sachet to contain the herbs during the bath. As you draw a warm bath, sprinkle the lavender directly into the water or allow the sachet to steep, letting the aromatic essence infuse the water.

Enhancing the herbal bath ritual with lavender can further involve creating a spa-like ambiance in the bathroom. Dim the lights to a soft glow, play calming music, and light a few candles or burn lavender-scented incense. These elements contribute to the overall immersive experience, turning your bath into a sanctuary where the soothing properties of lavender harmonize with the calming qualities of warm water.

Allow yourself to submerge into this aromatic haven, taking slow, deep breaths to fully absorb the calming effects. Lavender's gentle fragrance will envelop you, promoting relaxation and easing tension. The intentional setting, combined with the therapeutic properties of lavender, transforms the herbal bath into a sacred space—an oasis where the stress of the day washes away, leaving you rejuvenated in body and mind.

Safety and Harmony in Herbcraft

While nature's herbal gifts offer solace, it is crucial to tread with awareness and respect. Let these guidelines be your compass on this herbal journey:

Let the dance of chamomile, lavender, valerian, and their verdant companions linger in your heart. In teas, tinctures, capsules, or aromatic whispers, these herbs beckon us to embrace the gentle symphony of tranquility.

Safety and mindfulness become our cherished companions as we tread this herbal path. With each sip, each drop, and each fragrant inhale, may you find solace—a testament to the seamless dance between the natural world and the wellspring of human health. In the gentle arms of herbal remedies, we discover a tranquil sanctuary—a harmonious blend of nature's melodies and the resilient rhythm of the human spirit.

While herbs offer a natural and holistic approach to well-being, their potent compounds require careful consideration and respect.

Herb-Drug Interactions:

Herbs, like pharmaceutical medications, have the potential to interact with each other and with prescribed drugs. The expanded use of multiple herbs simultaneously may create synergistic or antagonistic effects. It is advisable to consult with healthcare professionals to understand potential interactions, especially if already taking medications.

Establishing a dialogue with healthcare providers ensures a comprehensive approach to well-being that considers both herbal remedies and conventional medical interventions. Providing a list of herbs being consumed, along with details of any medications, fosters open communication and allows for informed decision-making.

Individual Responses:

Individual responses to herbs can vary significantly. Factors such as age, pre-existing health conditions, allergies, and overall sensitivity play a role in how the body interacts with herbal compounds. Starting with low dosages and gradually increasing allows individuals to observe how their bodies respond to herbal remedies.

Maintaining a journal to document personal experiences with herbal consumption becomes a valuable tool. Recording any changes in mood, sleep patterns, or physical sensations provides insights into how specific herbs impact individual well-being. This self-awareness contributes to a mindful and tailored approach to herbal consumption.

Quality and Sourcing:

The quality of herbs used in herbal crafts significantly influences their efficacy and safety. Opting for organic, sustainably sourced herbs ensures that the herbal remedies crafted are free from pesticides, herbicides, and other contaminants. The expanded use of herbs underscores the importance of investing in high-quality botanicals.

Researching reputable sources for herbs, whether purchasing online or from local suppliers, becomes an integral aspect of herbal safety. Establishing relationships with trusted herbal suppliers ensures a consistent and reliable source of high-quality herbs. Certifications such as organic or fair trade further validate the quality of herbal products.

Pregnancy and Breastfeeding:

The expanded use of herbal remedies necessitates heightened awareness, especially during pregnancy and breastfeeding. Some herbs may have effects on fetal development or milk production. Seeking guidance from healthcare providers ensures that herbal choices align with the unique needs of expectant or nursing mothers.

Herbs such as chamomile, lavender, and ginger are generally considered safe during pregnancy, but individual responses vary. Engaging in open communication with healthcare professionals allows for personalized advice that considers both the potential benefits and risks of herbal consumption during these critical periods.

Monitoring for Side Effects:

Vigilance for any unexpected side effects or adverse reactions remains a cornerstone of responsible herbal consumption. While herbs are generally considered safe, certain individuals may experience sensitivities or allergic responses. Being attentive to changes in physical or mental well-being ensures a proactive response to potential side effects.

The expanded use of herbal remedies invites individuals to cultivate a heightened sense of self-awareness. Any persistent side effects, discomfort, or unfamiliar reactions warrant a pause in herbal consumption and prompt consultation with healthcare professionals. This vigilant approach prioritizes individual well-being and supports a safe and harmonious integration of herbs into daily life.

Professional Guidance:

The complexity of herbal interactions and individual health profiles underscores the importance of seeking professional guidance. Herbalists, naturopaths, and healthcare professionals with expertise in herbal medicine become invaluable partners in navigating the expanded landscape of herbal wellness.

Establishing a collaborative relationship with herbal practitioners involves open communication about health goals, existing conditions, and preferences. Herbal consultations provide an opportunity to receive personalized advice on herb selection, dosage, and potential interactions. This professional guidance ensures a holistic and informed approach to herbal well-being.

The Tapestry of Herbal Wellness: Crafting a Holistic Approach

The integration of herbs into daily life extends beyond functional use to become a mindful and intentional practice that encompasses physical, mental, and emotional well-being.

Mindful Consumption as a Ritual:

The expanded use of herbal remedies invites individuals to approach consumption as a ritual—a deliberate and intentional act of self-care. Whether sipping herbal teas, taking capsules or enjoying aromatherapy, each encounter with herbs becomes an opportunity for mindfulness. Engaging in the present moment, savoring the sensory experiences, and acknowledging the therapeutic journey contribute to the ritualistic nature of herbal consumption.

Mindful consumption involves cultivating a connection with the natural world and acknowledging the wisdom inherent in plants. The act of selecting herbs, preparing them with care, and savoring their effects becomes a ritualistic dance—a harmonious exchange between humans and the healing gifts of nature.

Cultivating Herbal Wisdom:

The expanded exploration of herbal remedies invites individuals to cultivate herbal wisdom—an understanding of the unique properties, benefits, and applications of various herbs. This wisdom extends beyond functional knowledge to include an appreciation for the cultural and historical significance of each herb.

Creating a personal herbal apothecary becomes a tangible expression of herbal wisdom. Organizing dried herbs, tinctures, and essential oils in a designated space reflects a commitment to holistic wellness. This curated collection of herbal allies serves as a visual reminder of the interconnectedness between humans and the plant kingdom.

Herbs as Allies in Holistic Wellness:

The expanded use of herbs positions them as allies in the broader tapestry of holistic wellness. Each herb, with its distinct properties, becomes a partner in supporting physical health, mental clarity, and emotional balance. The intentional selection and incorporation of specific herbs align with individual wellness goals and contribute to a multifaceted approach to health.

Crafting personalized herbal blends tailored to individual needs embodies the spirit of holistic wellness. Whether addressing stress, promoting sleep, or supporting cognitive function, herbs become versatile tools in the pursuit of overall well-being. The expanded use of herbs acknowledges their role as dynamic allies that adapt to the evolving needs of individuals.

Herbs and the Rhythms of Nature:

The expanded exploration of herbal remedies aligns with the inherent rhythms of nature. Herbs, as expressions of the natural world, invite individuals to attune themselves to seasonal cycles, lunar phases, and the ebb and flow of life. Integrating this awareness into herbal practices enhances the resonance between humans and the greater ecosystem.

Observing the seasonal availability of herbs and aligning their use with natural cycles fosters a sense of harmony. Herbs harvested or consumed during specific seasons may offer unique benefits that correspond to the energetics of that time. This attunement to nature's rhythms becomes a foundational aspect of holistic wellness.

Herbal Wellness as a Lifelong Journey:

The expanded use of herbal remedies unfolds as a lifelong journey—a continuous exploration of the vast and diverse world of plants. Embracing herbal wellness becomes a dynamic and evolving practice that adapts to the changing needs and circumstances of individuals. This journey extends beyond functional benefits to encompass a deepening relationship with the wisdom of plants.

Approaching herbal wellness as a lifelong journey involves a willingness to learn, experiment, and grow. Trying new herbs, exploring diverse herbal traditions, and sharing knowledge with others become integral aspects of this ongoing adventure. The expanded use of herbs serves as a reminder that herbal wellness is not a destination but a rich and fulfilling journey.

Embracing the Fullness of Herbal Serenity

The expanded exploration of herbal remedies unveils a tapestry of serenity that extends beyond mere functionality. The act of crafting herbal elixirs becomes a ritualistic dance, a mindful consumption practice, and a lifelong journey into the wisdom of plants. Each herb, with its unique virtues, contributes to the symphony of tranquility, supporting holistic wellness in the physical, mental, and emotional realms.

As individuals navigate the expanded landscape of herbal wellness, let them do so with reverence, awareness, and a deep connection to the rhythms of nature. The intentional use of herbs, guided by safety and professional counsel, becomes a testament to the seamless dance between humans and the healing gifts of the plant kingdom.

May the aromatic whispers of chamomile, the fragrant embrace of lavender, and the grounding touch of ashwagandha continue to weave their soothing notes into the fabric of daily life. In the gentle arms of herbal remedies, individuals discover not only relief from stress and anxiety but also a profound connection to the inherent wisdom of the natural world—a connection that enriches and sustains the holistic well-being of both body and soul.

Nurturing Harmony

Embarking on the journey to holistic well-being unveils the profound connection between our physical activities and the sanctuary of our mental health. In this exploration, we delve into the realm of physical approaches to reducing anxiety, recognizing the gentle symphony between body and mind. Join us as we navigate the benefits of exercise, the serene embrace of yoga and Tai Chi, and the pivotal role of restorative sleep in alleviating anxiety.

As with food and herbs, experiment with movement to find different ways to relieve anxiety and regulate hormones. There are as many ways to move the body as there are foods to eat.

Exercise as a Healing Balm

The dance of mind and body is exquisite; within this intricate choreography, physical activity emerges as a bridge. Regular exercise orchestrates the release of neurotransmitters like endorphins, serotonin, and dopamine—a symphony that harmonizes mood and dissipates stress. Its effects extend beyond the physical, weaving a tapestry of well-being.

Endorphins, those delightful "feel-good" companions, grace us during and after exercise. These natural mood enhancers bring euphoria, acting as gentle painkillers and lifting our spirits. In the rhythm of walking, jogging, cycling, or swimming, we find a surge of endorphins that become our allies in the journey to tranquility.

The heartbeat of regular physical activity regulates serotonin, the mood-stabilizing neurotransmitter often courted by medications for anxiety and depression. Exercise, a natural conductor of serotonin production, becomes a rhythmic dance leading to improved mood and a gentle reduction in anxiety.

Dopamine, the maestro of reward and pleasure, takes center stage during exercise. Its release creates a sense of accomplishment, weaving positive reinforcement into the tapestry of physical activity. This reward mechanism becomes a catalyst, inspiring us to maintain a consistent exercise routine, a rhythm that soothes the soul.

Against the canvas of stress, physical activity emerges as a powerful brushstroke, modulating cortisol—the body's stress hormone. Acute stress may momentarily elevate cortisol, but regular exercise nurtures adaptability, fostering effective cortisol regulation. This adaptive response becomes a shield, enhancing stress resilience over time.

The enchantment of exercise extends to the mind—a sharpening of memory, concentration, and problem-solving skills. In this cognitive ballet, anxiety management finds a partner, as a nimble mind navigates stressors with grace, preserving emotional well-being.

Group sports, fitness classes, and exercise groups create a canvas for social interaction. These connections, vital for mental health, offer emotional support and shared experiences. The fusion of physical activity and social engagement becomes a duet, reducing anxiety through the strength of shared moments.

The embrace of regular exercise extends to the realm of dreams, contributing to better sleep quality—an essential ally in anxiety management. As physical activity regulates circadian rhythms and encourages relaxation, the foundation for restful sleep is laid. With each night, sleep deepens, fortifying resilience against life's tribulations.

Some of the best exercises for anxiety reduction comes from the East: Yoga and Tai Chi

Within the ancient practice of yoga, physical postures, breath control, meditation, and mindfulness unite in a harmonious tapestry. This holistic approach becomes a sanctuary for stress and anxiety reduction. There are many ways to practice yoga, from gentle stretches to hot yoga that leave one exhausted and satiated. A few practices are listed here.

- Breath Awareness (Pranayama): Breath becomes the brushstroke in yoga's canvas. Techniques like deep breathing and alternate nostril breathing activate the body's relaxation response, an invitation to a tranquil state.

- Asanas (Poses): From gentle stretches to grounding postures, yoga becomes a ritual of physical relaxation and mental serenity. In poses like Child's Pose and Corpse Pose, a present-moment awareness unfurls, creating a haven of calm.

- Meditation and Mindfulness: Meditation and mindfulness practices intertwine with yoga, becoming tools for anxiety reduction. The mindful embrace of thoughts and sensations fosters non-judgmental acceptance of the present, guiding individuals through anxious moments.

- Yoga Nidra: The guided meditation of Yoga Nidra, or yogic sleep, beckons a deep relaxation. A systematic body scan and visualization become threads weaving a tapestry of calmness at both physical and mental levels.

Tai Chi for Flowing Tranquility:

Tai Chi, a Chinese martial art, emerges as a dance of slow, flowing movements and intentional breathwork. In its essence as "moving meditation," Tai Chi becomes a guide to balance, flexibility, and inner calm. As with yoga there are several types of Tai Chi to explore.

The choreographed movements of Tai Chi, slow and deliberate, beckon a focused and meditative state. This gentle dance becomes a balm, reducing stress and anxiety through intentional movement.

The heart of Tai Chi beats in the connection between movement, breath, and mental focus. This integration fosters an acute awareness of the present, paving a path to relaxation and mental clarity.

Tai Chi's routines often include elements of Qi Gong, a practice intertwining movement, breath, and meditation. Qi Gong, enhancing the flow of vital energy, becomes a source of balance and harmony.

Tai Chi's embrace is inclusive, welcoming individuals of all ages and fitness levels. Its low-impact nature invites those with physical limitations, offering an approach that enriches physical and mental well-being.

The Role of Sleep

Sleep and anxiety dance in a delicate duet—a bidirectional relationship where anxiety affects sleep, and disrupted sleep heightens anxiety. The restoration of sleep patterns becomes a cornerstone in anxiety management.

The artistry of sleep hygiene practices paints a canvas of improved sleep quality. Consistent sleep schedules, calming bedtime routines, cozy sleep environments, and minimized screen time create a symphony regulating circadian rhythms and nurturing restful sleep.

Embracing good sleep hygiene is like crafting a sanctuary for your well-being. It's an empowering journey that promises restful nights and brighter, more energized days. Let's explore these comforting principles:

- Revel in the beauty of a consistent sleep routine, allowing your body to dance with a natural rhythm every day- even on weekends.

- Indulge in a nightly pre-sleep ritual, a gentle invitation to tranquility that whispers to your body, "It's time to let go and embrace peace." Meditation, a hot bath, tea, or reading a (physical) book are ideas for your pre-sleep ritual. We will explore rituals in Chapter Eight.

- Transform your bedroom into a haven of serenity – a cool, dark cocoon where dreams unfold and your spirit finds solace.

- Treat yourself to the embrace of a cozy mattress and pillows, cocooning you in comfort as you drift into a sea of dreams.

- Bid adieu to the glow of screens, at least one hour before bedtime, allowing your mind to savor the soft hues of the evening and embrace the quietude of the night.

- Nourish your body wisely, savoring a light pre-sleep snack and choosing sustenance that nurtures rather than disrupts your nocturnal journey.

- Dance through the day with joyful movement, letting the echoes of your vitality linger into the night. Revel in the balance of energy and repose.

- If you seek the embrace of a nap, let it be a gentle caress of 20-30 minutes, a fleeting interlude that enhances rather than hinders your nightly rendezvous with dreams.

- Let natural light be your companion, a soothing melody for your circadian rhythm. Bask in its glow, allowing its warmth to guide your journey through day and night.

- Sip consciously, allowing your body to rest without interruptions. Invite stillness into your nights, a peaceful voyage through the quiet hours.

If after experimenting with sleep hygiene, food, and exercise, sleep is still elusive, remember that guidance awaits. Reach out to healthcare professionals, the guardians of dreams, who can help unveil the secrets to your most restful slumber.

By weaving these practices into your daily tapestry, you are crafting a haven where sleep becomes a cherished companion – a gentle and comforting voyage into the sanctuary of dreams.

With the symphony of physical activities and the restorative power of sleep, the path to well-being becomes a dance—a harmonious interplay of body and mind. May this journey be one of self-discovery, resilience, and the nurturing of harmony—an enduring ode to the holistic nature of human health and happiness.

Nurturing Tranquility

In our bustling world, where life races ahead, anxiety has become a common companion on the journey of mental well-being. Yet, within the realm of mindfulness and relaxation techniques, we find potent tools that gently guide us towards a haven of calm and presence. Join us on this exploration, where we uncover practical and accessible strategies, offering step-by-step guides to breathing exercises, simple meditations, and mindfulness practices—a roadmap to soothe the anxious soul. The breathing exercises can calm the mind and soothe the body within moments and are a gift for those having strong feelings and panic attacks.

Diaphragmatic Breathing (Deep Belly Breathing)

Let's embark on a journey of simplicity and effectiveness with diaphragmatic breathing. Find comfort in a seated or reclined position, hands resting on the chest and abdomen.

- Step 1: Find a Comfortable Position: Embrace comfort, sit, or lie down. Hands rest, one on your chest and the other on your abdomen.

- Step 2: Inhale Slowly Through Your Nose: Inhale deeply through your nose, let your abdomen expand, and feel your lungs fill from the bottom up.

- Step 3: Exhale Slowly Through Your Mouth: Exhale gently through your mouth, ensuring a longer exhale than your inhale.

- Step 4: Repeat: Engage in this rhythm for a few minutes. Gradually, let 5-10 minutes of diaphragmatic breathing become a daily ritual.

- Step 5: Embrace the Relaxation Response: This technique orchestrates relaxation by calming the "fight or flight" response and inviting the restful embrace of the parasympathetic nervous system.

- Step 6: Reflect on the Sensations: Take a moment to reflect on the sensations in your body, the calming effect on your mind, and the awareness of being grounded in the present.

This simple yet powerful exercise becomes a foundational practice for managing anxiety and fostering a connection between breath, body, and mind.

4-7-8 Breathing (Relaxing Breath):

Enter the dance of 4-7-8 breathing, a choreography of inhale, breath retention, and exhale—a soothing breath for the nervous system.

- Step 1: Sit or Lie Comfortably: Settle into comfort, and close your eyes if it feels right.

- Step 2: Inhale Quietly Through Your Nose for a Count of 4: Inhale serenely through your nose, counting to four.

- Step 3: Hold Your Breath for a Count of 7: Hold your breath in a gentle pause, counting to seven.

- Step 4: Exhale Completely Through Your Mouth for a Count of 8: Exhale gracefully through your mouth, creating a soft whooshing sound, counting to eight.

- Step 5: Repeat the Cycle: Engage in three more cycles, letting the numbers weave a tapestry of tranquility.

- Step 6: Sensory Awareness: Bring attention to the sensations during each phase of the breath—coolness as you inhale, the gentle pause, and the warm release during exhale.

This breathing technique becomes a melody, regulating breath, enhancing oxygen intake, and inviting the soothing presence of the parasympathetic nervous system.

Box Breathing (Square Breathing):

Step into the structure of box breathing, a balanced inhalation, breath retention, exhalation, and pause—a breath of intentional calm. Box Breathing is an excellent tool to use while in the midst of a panic attack. The balance of inhale, hold, exhale, hold, balances stress hormones and sends signals to your body that danger is no more.

- Step 1: Find a Comfortable Posture: Sit or stand comfortably, your back straight.

- Step 2: Inhale Slowly for a Count of 4: Inhale with purpose, counting steadily to four.

- Step 3: Hold Your Breath for a Count of 4: After inhaling, gently hold your breath for a count of four.

- Step 4: Exhale Slowly for a Count of 4: Release the breath slowly and completely through your mouth, counting to four.

- Step 5: Pause and Hold for a Count of 4: After exhaling, pause, and hold your breath for a count of four before beginning the next inhalation.

- Step 6: Repeat the Cycle: Continue the box breathing dance for several rounds, extending the duration as comfort allows.

- Step 7: Cultivate Mindful Focus: During the breath cycles, cultivate a mindful focus on the sensations of the breath and the rhythm of the counts.

This intentional approach to breathing becomes a structured ritual, fostering focus and a sense of calm.

Meditation and Mindfulness Practices

Meditation and mindfulness are not tools to use in the moment of anxiety, but habits that will decrease overall anxiety over time and bring health, joy, and awareness of the moment.

In the gentle art of body scan meditation, we bring our attention to different parts of the body, weaving awareness and relaxation into our being. Body scan meditation is a supportive way to ease into slumber. There are many free resources that have body scan meditation exercises for one to listen to and follow.

- Step 1: Find a Comfortable Position: Sit or lie down, close your eyes, and breathe deeply to center yourself.

- Step 2: Bring Attention to Your Toes: Begin with your toes, notice sensations, and with each breath, release tension.

- Step 3: Gradually Move Up the Body: Journey through each part, noticing warmth, tension, and sensations. Invite relaxation with every breath.

- Step 4: Be Present in Each Moment: Embrace the present in each moment, observing without judgment. If thoughts wander, gently guide them back to the present.

- Step 5: End with Full-Body Awareness: Conclude by uniting attention to your whole body, feeling the serenity spread.

- Step 6: Gentle Movements: Optionally, incorporate gentle movements or stretches after the body scan to further release any residual tension.

This meditation deepens body awareness, fosters relaxation, and establishes a mindful connection with the present.

Guided Visualization Meditation:

Enter the realm of guided visualization meditation—a creation of mental images that breathe peace, calm, and positivity into our minds. Guided meditation is a gentle relaxation tool that again can be found in many free or inexpensive online meditation resources.

- Step 1: Choose a Calming Scene: Select an image or scene of tranquility—a beach, a forest, a serene place.

- Step 2: Settle Into a Comfortable Position: Sit or lie down, close your eyes, and breathe deeply to center yourself.

- Step 3: Immerse Yourself in the Scene: Dive into the chosen scene, visualize the details, engage all senses, and sync your breath with the imagined environment.

- Step 4: Breathe and Relax: Inhale the positive elements, exhale tension, and let the calm of the scene infuse your being.

- Step 5: Stay Present in the Visualization: Linger in the guided visualization, letting peace wash over. Gently return to the present after a few minutes.

- Step 6: Journaling Reflections: Optionally, keep a journal to capture your reflections and any insights that emerge during or after the guided visualization.

This meditation guides the mind away from anxiety, creating a mental sanctuary of peace.

Mindful Breathing Meditation:

Enter the serene realm of mindful breathing meditation, focusing on breath as the anchor to present-moment awareness.

- Step 1: Find a Quiet Space: Sit undisturbed, close your eyes if comfortable.

- Step 2: Focus on Your Breath: Direct attention to your breath, noticing the sensations as you inhale and exhale.

- Step 3: Be Present in Each Breath: Allow your mind to dwell on each breath, guiding it back if it wanders. Notice the rhythm and flow.

- Step 4: Embrace Non-Judgmental Awareness: Let your awareness be non-judgmental. If distractions come, acknowledge without judgment, and return to the breath.

- Step 5: Set a Time Limit: Start with 5-10 minutes, extending gradually with familiarity.

- Step 6: Integrating Breath into Daily Activities: Extend the practice by bringing mindful breathing into daily activities, such as walking, working, or commuting.

This meditation nurtures present-moment awareness, calm, and the ability to remain anchored in the now.

Progressive Muscle Relaxation

1. Understanding Progressive Muscle Relaxation (PMR):

Progressive Muscle Relaxation (PMR) unfolds as a systematic dance of tension and release, an artful technique for both physical and mental relaxation.

- Step 1: Recognizing Muscle Tension: Begin by recognizing the presence of tension in your body. It might manifest as tightness, discomfort, or a subtle sense of unease.

- Step 2: Deepening Breath Awareness: Connect with your breath, deepening your inhalations and exhalations to enhance overall relaxation.

- Step 3: Systematic Muscle Engagement: Starting from your toes, consciously tense and then release each muscle group. Move gradually up your body—calves, thighs, abdomen, chest, arms, shoulders, neck, and face.

- Step 4: Mindful Observation: As you engage in this practice, observe the contrast between tension and relaxation. Cultivate a heightened awareness of your body's response.

- Step 5: Progressive Relaxation: Repeat the tension-release cycle for each muscle group, allowing the relaxation to deepen with each round.

- Step 6: Closing with Full-Body Relaxation: Conclude the session by letting go of any remaining tension, allowing your entire body to bask in a state of relaxation.

This practice fosters body awareness, diminishes muscle tension, and stands as a powerful technique for managing anxiety-induced physical symptoms. Although PMR will take about 20 minutes, it is a useful tool to use when overwhelmed with anxious thoughts.

In the tapestry of mindfulness and relaxation techniques, we discover accessible and effective tools for tending to anxiety—a gentle nurture of calm, presence, and self-awareness. Breathing exercises, meditation, and Progressive Muscle Relaxation become threads weaving a fabric of tranquility.

Incorporate these practices into daily life, empower yourself to actively manage mental well-being. Like any skill, proficiency grows with practice, and the benefits compound. Whether embraced independently or as part of a holistic anxiety management plan, these techniques offer steadfast companionship on the journey to cultivate calm and resilience in the face of life's challenges.

As you continue on this journey of nurturing tranquility, remember that the path is unique for each individual. Explore, adapt, and make these practices your own. May the gentle embrace of mindfulness and relaxation guide you to a place of inner serenity—a sanctuary where anxiety dissolves, and the present moment unfolds with grace and ease.

Embracing Hope

In the pursuit of holistic well-being, a comforting shift is unfolding as individuals increasingly turn to alternative therapies to navigate the complexities of anxiety. These approaches, deeply rooted in ancient traditions and practices, offer soothing perspectives on mental health and overall well-being. In this exploration, let's embark on a hopeful journey, uncovering the transformative potential within four alternative therapies—Acupuncture and Acupressure, Aromatherapy, Nature Therapy, and Tapping. Together, we'll understand how these gentle practices can be embraced as companions on the path to anxiety management.

Acupuncture and Acupressure

Let's begin our journey with the ancient Chinese healing practices of Acupuncture and Acupressure—time-honored traditions that have graced humanity for centuries, promoting balance and harmony within the body's energy systems. Enveloped in the philosophy of traditional Chinese medicine, these techniques view the body as a symphony of interconnected energy pathways, or meridians, through which the vital life force, known as qi, gracefully flows.

Acupuncture

Picture a tapestry of thin needles delicately inserted into specific points along the body's meridians. These points, like ancient secrets, correspond to energy centers, thought to influence the flow of qi, delicately addressing imbalances and ushering in overall well-being.

The placement of these acupuncture needles orchestrates a harmonious flow of qi, gently addressing blockages or deficiencies contributing to anxiety. It is a dance of energy that seeks to restore balance and alleviate the symphony of stress and tension.

In this dance, acupuncture whispers to the body, coaxing the release of endorphins—nature's own painkillers and mood enhancers. The specific points touched are like musical notes, playing a melody that resonates with relaxation and well-being.

Acupuncture extends a holistic embrace to health, recognizing the intricate dance between body and mind. While not a solitary remedy for anxiety, many find solace and support for their mental well-being through the rhythmic sessions of acupuncture.

Acupressure

Imagine a gentle dance of pressure, fingers or hands gracefully applying touch to specific points on the body, akin to acupuncture points but without the use of needles. This is the practice of Acupressure—where touch becomes a language of healing, stimulating these points to influence the flow of qi and usher in serenity.

Acupressure extends an invitation to self-application, a dance with oneself. Through simple techniques, like a gentle touch at the base of the skull or on the inner wrist, individuals can incorporate this dance into their daily routines, gracefully managing anxiety without the need for external intervention.

The dance of acupressure is known for its ability to reduce muscle tension, whispering relaxation to the body, and enhancing overall well-being. It is a non-invasive, natural approach to managing anxiety, its touch leaving behind a trail of tranquility.

As acupressure engages in its dance, the marriage with mindful breathing techniques enhances its beauty. Focusing on the breath while applying gentle pressure becomes a harmonious duet, calming the nervous system and alleviating anxiety.

Exercise: Calming Pressure Points

Point: Third Eye (Yin Tang):

- Location: Located between your eyebrows, in the indentation where the bridge of your nose meets the center of your forehead.

- Technique: Gently press with your thumb or index finger in a circular motion for about 1-2 minutes while taking slow, deep breaths. This point is believed to help calm the mind and alleviate stress.

Point: Union Valley (He Gu):

- Location: On the back of your hand, in the webbing between your thumb and index finger.

- Technique: Apply firm pressure and massage in a circular motion for 1-2 minutes. This point is associated with reducing tension and promoting relaxation.

Poimt: Inner Gate (Nei Guan):

- Location: On the inner side of your forearm, approximately three finger widths below the wrist crease.

- Technique: Press with your thumb in a circular or up-and-down motion for 1-2 minutes. This point is believed to calm the spirit and relieve anxiety.

Heavenly Pillar (Bai Hui):

- Location: At the top of your head, along the midline, in line with the tips of your ears.

- Technique: Gently press and massage in a circular motion for 1-2 minutes. This point is associated with promoting a sense of balance and tranquility.

Central Treasury (Zhong Wan):

- Location: Below the sternum, in the center of the abdomen.

- Technique: Apply gentle pressure with your fingertips in a circular motion for 1-2 minutes. This point is believed to calm the mind and soothe emotional distress.

Remember to breathe deeply and slowly as you perform these exercises. Feel free to adjust the pressure based on your comfort level and consult with a healthcare professional if you have any concerns or pre-existing conditions.

In the world of Acupuncture and Acupressure, ancient wisdom meets modern healing, providing holistic approaches to anxiety management. These practices, rooted in traditional Chinese medicine, acknowledge the interconnected dance of physical and mental well-being, offering individuals tools to foster balance and resilience.

Aromatherapy

Now, let's step into the enchanting realm of Aromatherapy—a therapeutic dance with the aromatic compounds of essential oils, each drop carrying the promise of enhanced physical and mental well-being. The inhalation or gentle application of these oils becomes a dance of healing, a comforting alternative therapy for those seeking relief from anxiety.

Essential Oils for Anxiety:

- Lavender: Envision fields of lavender, renowned for their calming properties. The scent of lavender, like a gentle lullaby, has the power to reduce anxiety levels, promote relaxation, and tenderly improve sleep quality. Whether diffused, applied topically, or added to a bath, lavender oil becomes a fragrant remedy.

- Chamomile: Enter the embrace of chamomile, its soothing and anti-anxiety effects a balm for the soul. The aroma of chamomile, like a whispered promise, alleviates stress and nurtures tranquility. Diffusing chamomile oil or adding it to a carrier oil becomes a ritual of self-care.

- Bergamot: Picture the zest of bergamot oranges, their uplifting and mood-enhancing properties dancing through the air. The citrusy aroma of bergamot, a burst of sunshine, is believed to reduce stress and anxiety. Aromatherapy with bergamot oil is an art, creating a positive and energizing atmosphere.

- Frankincense: Step into the mystique of frankincense, its grounding and centering effects weaving a tapestry of calm. Inhaling the scent of frankincense, a timeless dance, induces serenity and promotes mindfulness. Diffusing frankincense oil or adding a few drops to a personal inhaler is a poetic application.

- Ylang-Ylang: Embrace the exotic allure of ylang-ylang, known for its euphoric and balancing qualities. The sweet and floral fragrance of ylang-ylang is believed to reduce tension and uplift the spirit. Incorporating ylang-ylang oil into your self-care routine, whether through diffusion or blending with a carrier oil, adds a touch of exotic tranquility to your anxiety management practices.

Each of these essential oils offers a unique olfactory journey, contributing to a holistic approach to anxiety relief. Experiment with different oils or create your own blends to discover the scents that resonate most with you on your journey to well-being.

Methods of Application:

- Diffusion: Imagine the gentle diffusion of essential oils, a mist carrying their essence throughout a space. Essential oil diffusers become vessels of therapeutic scents, creating an atmosphere of serenity.

- Topical Application: Envision the tender touch of essential oils on the skin, diluted in a carrier oil. Wrist, temples, or the back of the neck become canvases for the application, a dance of fragrant self-care.

- Inhalation: Inhale the scents directly from the bottle or through a tissue, the dance of aromas enveloping the senses. Personal inhalers or diffuser jewelry become portable companions in this aromatic journey.

- Baths: Picture a warm bath, essential oils mingling with the water, creating a sensory-rich experience. The combination of warm water and the inhalation of essential oils becomes a dance of relaxation and stress reduction. Here is a simple bath recipe:

Soothing Lavender and Chamomile Essential Oil Bath

Ingredients:

- 1 cup Epsom salt

- 10 drops lavender essential oil

- 5 drops chamomile essential oil

- 1/2 cup baking soda (optional for additional skin softening)

Instructions:

Prepare the Bath:

- Fill your bathtub with warm water. Ensure the temperature is comfortable for you.

Add Epsom Salt:

- Pour 1 cup of Epsom salt into the running water. Epsom salt can help relax muscles and promote a sense of calm.

Incorporate Essential Oils:

- Add 10 drops of lavender essential oil and 5 drops of chamomile essential oil to the bathwater. These oils are known for their calming and soothing properties.

Optional: Baking Soda:

- If desired, add 1/2 cup of baking soda to the water. Baking soda can contribute to skin softening.

Swirl and Mix:

- Swirl the water gently to mix the essential oils and Epsom salt evenly.

Create a Relaxing Atmosphere:

- Dim the lights, play soft music, or light a few candles to enhance the relaxing ambiance of your bath.

Soak and Breathe:

- Immerse yourself in the bath, taking slow, deep breaths. Allow the calming scents of lavender and chamomile to envelop you.

Relaxation Time:

- Stay in the bath for at least 20-30 minutes to fully experience the soothing effects.

After Bath Care:

- Pat your skin dry with a towel and follow up with your favorite moisturizer if needed.

This essential oil bath is designed to promote relaxation, ease tension, and provide a sensory-rich experience. Adjust the essential oil quantities based on your preference, and feel free to explore other calming essential oils like bergamot, frankincense, or ylang-ylang. Always be cautious with essential oils, especially if you have skin sensitivities, and consult with a healthcare professional if needed. Enjoy your calming and rejuvenating bath.

Mind-Body Connection:

- Association with Positive Experiences: Aromatherapy unfolds as a dance with the mind-body connection, linking scents with positive experiences. The olfactory system, intimately connected to the limbic system, orchestrates an emotional symphony. Certain scents become notes of comfort, relaxation, or joy.

- Calming the Nervous System: The inhalation of calming essential oils engages in a dance with the nervous system, reducing the activity of the "fight or flight" response and enhancing the restful "rest and digest" state. This ballet of scents contributes to anxiety reduction.

- Individual Variability: In this dance of aromas, individual responses vary. What brings calm to one might not resonate with another. Exploring different essential oils, attuning to personal preferences, amplifies the effectiveness of aromatherapy.

In the realm of Aromatherapy, the dance of scents becomes a therapeutic journey, engaging the mind, body, and senses in a harmonious rhythm. Essential oils, like fragrant notes, offer an alternative therapy for anxiety relief, creating a dance that awakens a deeper connection to oneself and the world.

Nature Therapy

Now, let's step into the nurturing embrace of Nature Therapy—a therapeutic dance with the natural world, where the rustle of leaves and the gentle caress of a breeze become healers. Nature's tender touch has been recognized across cultures and time, offering profound insights into the holistic dance of mental well-being.

Benefits of Nature Therapy for Anxiety:

- Stress Reduction: Nature therapy unfolds as a dance with stress reduction, a symphony of greenery lowering cortisol levels, the stress hormone. In nature's arms, a sense of calm descends.

- Improved Mood: The dance with nature paints emotions in hues of happiness, contentment, and relaxation. The sensory richness of natural environments becomes strokes on the canvas of a positive mood.

- Enhanced Cognitive Function: Nature therapy choreographs an intricate dance of improved cognitive function, where attention and creativity take center stage. The restorative theory whispers that nature's embrace alleviates mental fatigue and refines focus.

- Connection to the Present Moment: Nature is a dance that promotes mindfulness, a gentle reminder to be present. The sights, sounds, and sensations of nature engage the senses, offering a mindful reprieve from anxious thoughts.

Ways to Engage in Nature Therapy:

Forest Bathing (Shinrin-Yoku):

Visualize a dance with trees, known as Forest Bathing or Shinrin-Yoku. It is an immersive and intentional practice that transcends the simple act of taking a walk in the woods. When engaging in Forest Bathing, every step becomes a mindful connection with nature's rhythm. The forest, in all its splendor, transforms into a living sanctuary, offering more than just a scenic backdrop.

As you wander through the woods during a Forest Bathing session, let the rustling leaves be your whispered companions, and the dappled sunlight filtering through the branches your guide. The air, infused with the earthy perfume of moss and pine, becomes a sensory symphony that resonates with tranquility. The ground beneath your feet, a natural carpet of fallen leaves and soft soil, invites you to tread gently and feel the Earth's embrace.

Immerse yourself in the intricate details of the forest—the delicate ferns unfurling in hidden corners, the vibrant mushrooms peeking through the underbrush, and the symmetrical patterns of sunlight playing on the forest floor. Each element, a testament to the resilience and interconnectedness of the natural world, becomes a source of wonder and grounding.

Forest Bathing encourages you to engage not just with the visual beauty of the surroundings but also with the textures, scents, and sounds that envelop you. Run your fingers along the rough bark of an ancient tree, inhale deeply the aroma of damp soil after a gentle rain, and listen to the symphony of bird songs and rustling leaves overhead. These moments of sensory connection create a profound sense of presence and mindfulness.

Allow the forest to be your guide in the art of slowing down. As you find a quiet spot, perhaps beside a babbling brook or under a canopy of ancient trees, let the stillness seep into your being. Close your eyes and absorb the symphony of nature around you. In these moments of quiet reflection, you may sense the subtle yet powerful healing energies that emanate from the heart of the forest.

Forest Bathing is more than a leisurely stroll; it is a deliberate and therapeutic communion with nature. Research suggests that this practice can reduce stress, lower blood pressure, and boost overall well-being. By fostering a deep connection with the natural world, Forest Bathing becomes a transformative journey—one where the forest becomes not just a backdrop but an active participant in your quest for inner peace and harmony.

- Nature Walks: Imagine a simple nature walk, a dance with greenery that unfolds in parks, nature reserves, or any inviting green space. The gentle rhythm of walking enhances the therapeutic benefits.

- Gardening: Picture hands in the soil, a dance with the earth through gardening. Planting, nurturing, and witnessing growth become fulfilling and grounding movements.

- Outdoor Meditation: Envision meditation taking root in the embrace of the great outdoors, where the natural world becomes an integral part of your contemplative journey. This practice transcends the traditional notion of sitting in silence; instead, it invites you to become an active participant in the rhythmic dance between your inner self and the living symphony of nature.

As you find a serene spot for outdoor meditation, whether under the shade of a mighty tree, by the side of a babbling brook, or on a tranquil hilltop, let the surroundings become an extension of your meditation cushion. The gentle rustle of leaves overhead becomes a whispered mantra, a rhythmic reminder of the interconnectedness of all things. The fragrance of blooming flowers or the earthy scent of the soil beneath you becomes the incense, subtly guiding you into a state of heightened awareness.

Close your eyes and attune your senses to the world around you. Feel the warmth of the sun on your skin, the cool breeze playing with your hair, and the solid support of the ground beneath you. In outdoor meditation, nature becomes your co-meditator, offering its own wisdom in the form of ambient sounds, scents, and sensations.

As you delve into the stillness, allow the sounds of nature to anchor your focus. The chirping of birds, the babbling of a nearby stream, or the distant rustle of wildlife—all become threads in the tapestry of your meditation. Rather than distractions, these natural sounds become gateways to a deeper state of mindfulness, connecting you to the present moment.

Let your awareness expand beyond your breath and bodily sensations to include the larger ecosystem around you. Notice the play of light and shadow as leaves sway in the wind, or the way the colors of the landscape shift with the movement of the sun. The outdoor meditation experience is a multisensory immersion, encouraging you to be fully present in the ever-changing canvas of nature.

Incorporate mindful walking into your outdoor meditation practice. As you move through the natural environment, let each step be a conscious connection with the Earth. Feel the textures beneath your feet, whether it's soft grass, cool stones, or the warmth of sun-soaked earth. Walking becomes a moving meditation, a harmonious dance between your breath, your steps, and the living, breathing world around you.

Outdoor meditation transcends the boundaries of traditional practices, offering a holistic and immersive experience. Research suggests that spending time in nature and practicing mindfulness outdoors can lead to increased feelings of well-being, reduced stress levels, and a heightened sense of connection to the environment. In this dance of inner peace and nature's embrace, outdoor meditation becomes a profound journey into the heart of mindfulness.

- Nature Retreats: Envision retreats or getaways in natural settings, a prolonged dance with nature. Hiking, camping, or simply savoring the tranquility become acts of self-care.

Biophilia Hypothesis:

Dive into the profound concept of our innate connection to nature—a dance that transcends time and is deeply embedded in the fabric of human existence. The biophilia hypothesis, coined by biologist E.O. Wilson, illuminates the idea that humans, as a product of evolution, possess an inherent affinity for the natural world. This intrinsic bond is not merely a passing fancy; it is a fundamental aspect of our being, a dance partner that profoundly influences our physical, mental, and emotional well-being.

At the core of the biophilia hypothesis is the recognition that throughout our evolutionary journey, our ancestors developed in harmony with the natural environment. The sights, sounds, and rhythms of nature were constant companions, shaping the very essence of what it means to be human. As a result, our biology is intricately entwined with the dance of the natural world, and our well-being is intrinsically linked to the health of the ecosystems that surround us.

Imagine this dance of nature as a timeless duet, where the rustle of leaves, the babbling of streams, and the symphony of bird songs are notes in a melody that resonates with our core. The green hues of forests, the vastness of open landscapes, and the soothing blue of sky and water become a visual poetry that speaks to the very soul of our existence. In recognizing this connection, we acknowledge that nature is not a separate entity but an integral part of who we are.

As urbanization and modern lifestyles increasingly pull us away from the natural dance, there is a growing awareness of the profound impact this disconnection can have on our well-being. Studies suggest that restoring this innate connection to nature, whether through spending time outdoors, immersing ourselves in natural settings, or simply cultivating indoor spaces with elements of nature, can have remarkable effects on our mental and physical health.

Rekindling our innate connection to nature becomes a transformative act—a conscious choice to re-enter the dance that has been ongoing for millennia. This dance is not a luxury but a necessity, a vital rhythm that sustains our holistic well-being. As we embrace our biophilic nature, we rediscover a source of solace, inspiration, and resilience—a dance partner that has been patiently waiting for us to return to the harmonious flow of life.

- Urban Nature: Even in urban landscapes, the dance with nature unfolds. Green spaces, parks, or potted plants become partners in the urban dance of nature therapy, offering opportunities for positive mental health outcomes.

- Restorative Environments: Picture restorative environments, where nature's dance replenishes cognitive resources and eases mental fatigue. The green backdrop becomes a canvas for the mind to unwind and rejuvenate.

Tapping

Tapping into Emotional Freedom: (EFT)

Lastly, let's explore the unique dance of Tapping—a therapeutic approach that intertwines ancient Chinese acupressure with the elegance of modern psychology. Tapping becomes a dance with the body's meridian points, a rhythm that harmonizes thoughts and emotions to alleviate anxiety and emotional challenges.

The EFT Process:

Begin this dance by identifying the specific issue or emotion causing distress. It might be anxiety, stress, fear, or any emotion that calls for acknowledgment.

In the dance of Tapping, craft a setup statement. This is a verbal acknowledgment of the issue paired with a self-acceptance affirmation. It's a compassionate dance of words, such as "Even though I feel anxious about [specific situation], I deeply and completely accept myself."

Now, imagine a dance with the body's meridian points—top of the head, eyebrow, side of the eye, under the eye, under the nose, chin, collarbone, and under the arm. This sequence is accompanied by short phrases related to the issue. It's a dance of words and touch, gradually shifting from the negative to positive affirmations.

Specific Tapping Points:

1. Top of the Head: Picture a circle or dot at the crown of the head.

2. Eyebrow: Mark a point along the eyebrow line, right where the eyebrow begins.

3. Side of the Eye: Indicate a spot on the bone at the outer corner of the eye.

4. Under the Eye: Identify a point on the bone just below the eye, towards the nose.

5. Under the Nose: Mark a spot above the upper lip, right below the nose.

6. Chin: Highlight a point on the chin, in the center.

7. Collarbone: Indicate a point on each side of the chest, where the collarbone meets the breastbone.

8. Under the Arm: Mark a point about four inches below the armpit.

Connect these points in the order mentioned to represent the Tapping Sequence. You might envision lines or arrows connecting them in a sequence to guide the tapping process. As you tap each point, you can also accompany it with positive affirmations related to the issue you're addressing.

Remember, this is a mental representation, and you can adapt it based on your preferences. The key is to tap each point gently and deliberately while focusing on the specific issue and gradually transitioning to more positive thoughts.

- Check-in: After this rhythmic dance, check in with your emotional intensity. The goal is to feel a reduction in the intensity of the negative emotion, a shift toward a more balanced and positive state.

- Repeat if Necessary: In this dance, some find relief after one round, while others may need an encore. Repeat the tapping sequence with adjusted setup statements until the emotional distress waltzes away.

The Science of Tapping:

Tapping has the power to reduce cortisol levels, signaling a decrease in stress. The rhythmic dance on acupressure points, paired with verbal expression, becomes a calming melody for the nervous system.

Research suggests that tapping orchestrates changes in brainwave patterns. In particular, it diminishes hyper-arousal in the amygdala, the emotional processing hub of the brain. This dance contributes to the observed calming and desensitizing effects.

Tapping becomes a dance with neuroplasticity—the brain's ability to rewire itself. The physical tapping, combined with focused attention on thoughts and emotions, weaves a transformative dance, facilitating a shift in neural pathways linked to negative emotions.

In this therapeutic dance, tapping joins hands with other anxiety management techniques. It seamlessly integrates into daily routines, becoming a self-help tool for addressing both acute and chronic emotional challenges.

In the enchanting realm of alternative therapies for anxiety, a hopeful dance unfolds—a dance that acknowledges the interconnectedness of the mind, body, and environment. Acupuncture and Acupressure engage with ancient Chinese wisdom, a dance with energy systems to alleviate anxiety. Aromatherapy, a dance of scents and sensations, captivates the mind-body connection through the therapeutic power of essential oils. Nature therapy, a dance with the great outdoors, harmonizes stress reduction, mood improvement, and enhanced cognitive function. Tapping, a rhythmic dance with meridian points, offers a unique and transformative journey to emotional freedom.

As individuals seek comprehensive and personalized approaches to anxiety management, these alternative therapies extend a comforting hand—a hand that holds valuable tools for self-care. Integrating these dances into daily routines empowers individuals to explore diverse avenues for relaxation, resilience, and a sense of balance. An open mind becomes the dance partner, recognizing that each individual responds uniquely. Combining these practices with conventional approaches and seeking guidance from healthcare professionals ensures a comprehensive and tailored waltz toward anxiety relief. Embracing the richness of alternative therapies becomes a dance, contributing to a holistic journey toward mental well-being and a deeper connection to oneself and the world. Dance on, embracing the hope within each step.

Nurturing Your Path to Lasting Serenity

Embarking on a journey to manage anxiety is an intricate dance—one that involves recognizing the nuances of your mind, the whispers of your body, and the rhythm of your lifestyle. In this guide, we invite you to weave a tapestry of lasting well-being through a personalized anxiety management plan. Together, we'll explore the gentle integration of natural remedies, lifestyle adjustments, and self-monitoring strategies to create an antidote for tranquility that extends beyond mere symptom relief.

Crafting Your Antidote: A Holistic Approach

1. Harmony in Natural Remedies:

The creation of your personalized anxiety management plan is a symphony of self-care, incorporating the wisdom from acupressure, aromatherapy, nature therapy, and tapping. Imagine crafting your daily rituals as moments of self-love and resilience.

- Morning Serenity: As the sun rises, gift yourself a brief acupressure session, a tender touch on points like the base of your skull. Inhale the invigorating scent of bergamot essential oil, letting it dance through your senses. This is your morning serenade—a harmonious start to the day.

- Midday Resilience: Amid the hustle, tap into your resilience with personalized tapping sequences. Let the soothing aroma of lavender or chamomile be a calming breeze through your day. A personal inhaler becomes a portable sanctuary, offering moments of tranquility in the palm of your hand.

- Nature's Embrace: Carve time for nature therapy, whether a brief stroll or a weekend retreat. Nature becomes your co-creator, infusing each step with its healing touch. The dance with the outdoors is a powerful complement to your holistic journey.

- Evening Serenity: As the day gently fades, indulge in an evening acupressure routine. Allow the scent of lavender or frankincense to guide you into relaxation. A tapping session becomes a lullaby for a calm and restful night. This is your evening serenity—an exquisite closure to the day.

2. Lifestyle Changes for Radiant Well-being:

Beyond immediate relief, lasting well-being emerges from lifestyle changes—a transformation of daily habits and self-nurturing practices.

- Nutritional Symphony: Explore foods that dance with your well-being. Omega-3-rich delights like salmon and walnuts join this nutritional symphony, offering notes of mood regulation. Minimize caffeine and sugar, inviting a serene cadence to your dietary choices.

- Movement as Poetry: Embrace exercise as a poetic dance for your body and mind. Feel the rhythm of endorphins as you move, releasing stress in the embrace of nature or a favorite workout space. This is the dance of "exercise as medicine," a love letter to your mental health.

- Dreamy Repose: Prioritize quality sleep as a nightly ritual. Create a dreamy atmosphere, gently letting go of the day's tensions. Consistent sleep becomes the melody of emotional regulation, harmonizing with your quest for well-being.

- Mindful Melodies: Infuse mindfulness into your daily composition. Breathe in the melodies of mindfulness—meditation, breathing exercises, and progressive muscle relaxation. These practices become interludes, weaving a present-moment awareness into the fabric of your days.

- Harmony of Connection: Cultivate meaningful social connections, recognizing their role as vital notes in your life's melody. Engage in activities that resonate with your soul, a communal dance that dispels feelings of isolation and amplifies your joy.

- Holistic Healing: Explore complementary therapies like acupuncture and massage, harmonizing with traditional healthcare professionals. This collaboration ensures your plan is a rich tapestry, woven with expertise and tailored to your unique journey.

3. Measuring Progress and Embracing Adaptability:

Crafting your personalized anxiety management plan is a dynamic dance, requiring self-awareness, reflection, and an openness to adaptation.

- Journal of Reflection: Keep a journal, a canvas for your thoughts, emotions, and the dance of natural remedies.

Explore the techniques in this book and note the ones you enjoy, and the ones that are less helpful. Recall that some exercises will ease anxiety symptoms immediately and others will need space and time to work their soothing magic. Observe patterns, celebrate victories, and note areas for refinement. This journal is a mirror reflecting the evolving artwork of your well-being.

- Self-Discovery Assessment: Periodically assess your well-being using self-assessment tools. These checkpoints offer clarity on your journey, guiding you to adjust steps and refine your dance. Reputable resources online provide gentle guidance in this self-discovery.

- Consultation with Guides: Regularly consult with healthcare professionals, your guides on this journey. Share your progress, welcome their insights, and ensure your plan aligns with your overarching health goals. This collaboration becomes a chorus of support.

- Echoes of Support: Engage with your support system, allowing their perspectives to echo in your self-awareness. Friends, family, or a therapist contribute valuable observations, enhancing your understanding and illuminating potential areas for growth.

- Fluidity of Well-being: Recognize that personalization is an ongoing dance. Be receptive to new remedies, adjust lifestyle practices, and embrace feedback. Flexibility and adaptability are your partners, ensuring your plan remains a fluid and effective expression of your pursuit of well-being.

In the symphony of crafting your personalized anxiety management plan, every note is a promise—a promise of self-discovery, resilience, and lasting serenity. This journey is a dance of hope, an ode to your well-being. As you embrace each step, let hope guide your rhythm, and may your dance be one of joy and profound self-care. The canvas is yours—paint it with the colors of tranquility.

Cultivating Serenity with Natural Remedies and Compassionate Self-Care

In the intricate fabric of mental well-being, anxiety weaves its threads, impacting lives in nuanced ways. Throughout this exploration, we've immersed ourselves in a spectrum of natural remedies, lifestyle adjustments, and self-care practices that collectively craft a holistic approach to taming anxiety. As we wrap up this journey, let's revisit the potential of natural remedies, underscore the importance of continual self-care, and extend a hand toward additional resources for those seeking to deepen their understanding of these soothing remedies.

Natural remedies for anxiety extend beyond mere symptom relief; they embody a holistic philosophy that embraces the unity of mind, body, and environment. From the ancient wisdom of acupressure and acupuncture to the enchanting scents of aromatherapy, the revitalizing touch of nature therapy, and the rhythmic tapping of Emotional Freedom Technique (EFT), these approaches provide accessible tools for navigating the intricate landscape of anxiety.

- Acupressure and Acupuncture: Rooted in ancient Chinese wisdom, these practices restore balance by engaging with the body's energy systems. Tapping into specific points fosters a tangible connection between physical touch and emotional well-being, offering a pathway to relaxation and anxiety alleviation.

- Aromatherapy: Harnessing the power of scent, aromatherapy uses essential oils to evoke emotional responses and promote mental well-being. Scents like lavender, chamomile, bergamot, and frankincense invite individuals on a sensory journey, influencing mood and gently reducing anxiety.

- Nature Therapy: Beyond aesthetics, nature therapy has proven its healing power in stress reduction, mood enhancement, and cognitive rejuvenation. Whether through immersive forest bathing, nature walks, gardening, or outdoor meditation, nature therapy provides a profound connection to the natural world, offering solace and balance.

- Tapping (Emotional Freedom Technique - EFT): This unique blend of ancient acupressure principles and modern psychology empowers individuals in their pursuit of emotional freedom. By tapping on specific meridian points while acknowledging emotions, individuals navigate anxiety and other emotional challenges, fostering a sense of empowerment.

These natural remedies, when woven into a personalized anxiety management plan, offer an array of benefits. From immediate relief to the cultivation of long-term resilience, these approaches honor the complexity of individual experiences while providing valuable tools for navigating the ebbs and flows of mental well-being.

Encouraging Gentle Self-Care and a Tender Focus on Mental Health:

Crafting a personalized anxiety management plan isn't a one-time task; it's an ongoing, dynamic process. Embracing self-care as a daily ritual contributes to the overall well-being of mind and body. The strategies explored here—whether they involve acupressure points, moments of immersion in nature, or the subtle embrace of aromatherapy—invite individuals to be active participants in their mental health journey.

- Mindful Integration: Weaving natural remedies into daily routines establishes a sense of continuity and mindfulness. Consistency becomes a gentle companion, and small, intentional acts of self-care cumulatively contribute to a resilient and balanced mental state.

- Holistic Lifestyle: Beyond natural remedies, lifestyle changes play a pivotal role in anxiety management. Adopting a diet rich in mood-regulating nutrients, prioritizing regular exercise, ensuring quality sleep, and fostering social connections collectively support a holistic approach to mental well-being.

- Mindfulness Practices: Cultivating mindfulness through practices like meditation, deep breathing, and progressive muscle relaxation enhances self-awareness. These practices serve as anchors in the present moment, mitigating the impact of anxious thoughts and promoting a sense of inner calm.

- Adaptability and Flexibility: Recognizing that mental health is a dynamic journey encourages an adaptable and flexible approach. Just as individuals evolve, so should their anxiety management plan. Being open to adjustments, exploring new strategies, and seeking professional guidance when needed contribute to a resilient and responsive self-care routine.

In the symphony of crafting your personalized anxiety management plan, every note is not just a promise but a commitment to your well-being. This journey is a dance of hope, an ode to resilience and lasting serenity. As you embrace each step, let hope guide your rhythm, and may your dance be one of joy and profound self-care. The canvas is yours—paint it with the colors of tranquility, and let the music of your well-being resonate through every facet of your life.

In the intricate fabric of mental well-being, anxiety weaves its threads, impacting lives in nuanced ways. Throughout this extended exploration, we've delved into the richness of natural remedies, the transformative power of lifestyle adjustments, and the profound impact of self-care practices that collectively craft a holistic approach to taming anxiety. As we conclude this extended journey, let's reflect on the potential of natural remedies, reemphasize the importance of continual self-care, and provide additional resources for those seeking to deepen their understanding of these soothing remedies.

Natural remedies for anxiety embody a holistic philosophy that recognizes the interconnectedness of mind, body, and environment. From the ancient wisdom of acupressure and acupuncture to the enchanting scents of aromatherapy, the revitalizing touch of nature therapy, and the rhythmic tapping of Emotional Freedom Technique (EFT), these approaches offer accessible tools for navigating the complex landscape of anxiety.

- Acupressure and Acupuncture: Rooted in ancient Chinese wisdom, these practices are gateways to restoring balance by engaging with the body's energy systems. The dance of touch and meridian points fosters a tangible connection between physical well-being and emotional equilibrium.

- Aromatherapy: Harnessing the power of scent, aromatherapy becomes an art of emotional alchemy. Essential oils like lavender, chamomile, bergamot, and frankincense transform the sensory landscape, influencing mood and gently guiding individuals toward a state of reduced anxiety.

- Nature Therapy: Beyond aesthetics, nature therapy transcends into a healing modality that impacts stress, mood, and cognitive function. Whether through immersive forest bathing, nature walks, gardening, or outdoor meditation, nature therapy becomes a profound connection to the natural world, offering solace and balance.

- Tapping (Emotional Freedom Technique - EFT): This unique blend of ancient acupressure principles and modern psychology empowers individuals in their pursuit of emotional freedom. By tapping on specific meridian points while acknowledging emotions, individuals navigate anxiety and other emotional challenges, fostering a sense of empowerment and control.

These natural remedies, woven into the fabric of a personalized anxiety management plan, offer an array of benefits. From immediate relief to the cultivation of long-term resilience, these approaches honor the complexity of individual experiences while providing valuable tools for navigating the ebbs and flows of mental well-being.

In this extended exploration, the fluidity of your well-being journey is illuminated, showcasing the beauty of adaptability and the strength found in embracing new remedies. As you engage in the dance of hope, may your personalized anxiety management plan be a living testament to resilience, self-discovery, and lasting serenity. The canvas is yours—paint it with the colors of tranquility, and let the music of your well-being resonate through every facet of your life.

Remember, each individual's journey is unique, and seeking guidance from healthcare professionals is crucial. These resources complement your journey, providing additional insights and perspectives on holistic well-being.

As we conclude this extended exploration, may the dance of hope and self-care continue to guide your steps. Your well-being is a masterpiece in progress, and the canvas of tranquility awaits your creative touch. Embrace the wisdom of natural remedies, cultivate compassionate self-care, and let the journey toward lasting serenity unfold—one intentional step at a time.

Guiding You Deeper into the World of Natural Anxiety Remedies:

Empowering individuals on their journey to a deeper understanding of natural anxiety remedies involves providing an expansive array of resources. Whether you seek additional information, specific techniques, or professional support, the following resources offer a comprehensive exploration of natural remedies for anxiety:

1. Books:

- "The Complete Guide to Acupressure" by I. Smith

- "The Healing Intelligence of Essential Oils" by Kurt Schnaubelt

- "The Nature Fix: Why Nature Makes Us Happier, Healthier, and More Creative" by Florence Williams

- "The Tapping Solution" by Nick Ortner

- "The Spark in the Machine" by Dr. Daniel Keown

- "The Fragrant Mind" by Valerie Ann Worwood

2. Websites and Organizations:

- [Acupuncture Today](https://www.acupuncturetoday.com/): An invaluable resource for information on acupuncture and related practices.

- [National Association for Holistic Aromatherapy (NAHA)](https://naha.org/): Offers in-depth information on aromatherapy, including educational resources, research articles, and practitioner directories.

- [Association of Nature and Forest Therapy Guides and Programs](https://www.natureandforesttherapy.org/): Provides a wealth of resources on forest therapy, including certified guides, research articles, and upcoming events.

- [The Tapping Solution](https://www.thetappingsolution.com/): A comprehensive resource on tapping, offering guidance, videos, practitioner directories, and an extensive blog.

3. Apps:

- [Insight Timer](https://insighttimer.com/): A versatile app offering a variety of guided meditations, mindfulness exercises, and breathing techniques, fostering a sense of calm and focus.

- [Calm](https://www.calm.com/): Features guided meditations, sleep stories narrated by soothing voices, and relaxation exercises, promoting a tranquil mind and restful sleep.

- [Headspace](https://www.headspace.com/): A meditation app providing mindfulness exercises, sleep aids, and stress-relief techniques, suitable for beginners and experienced practitioners alike.

4. Professional Support:

- Seek guidance from licensed acupuncturists, aromatherapists, and nature therapy guides for personalized assistance tailored to your unique needs.

- Consult mental health professionals, including therapists, counselors, and psychologists, for comprehensive support in addressing anxiety and promoting overall well-being.

In conclusion, the journey toward anxiety management is a nuanced and evolving expedition. Natural remedies, when seamlessly integrated into a holistic approach, provide a rich tapestry of tools for individuals to weave into their daily lives. Embracing ongoing self-care, remaining attuned to mental health, and exploring an abundance of resources for further exploration empower individuals to navigate the currents of anxiety with resilience and mindfulness. As we continue to unravel the complexities of mental well-being, may each step toward well-being be guided by compassion, self-discovery, and the transformative power of natural remedies.

www.ingramcontent.com/pod-product-compliance
Lightning Source LLC
LaVergne TN
LVHW021829060526
838201LV00058B/3570